The Complete Works of Ricardo Reis

The Complete Works of Ricardo Reis

Fernando Pessoa

Edited by Jerónimo Pizarro & Jorge Uribe

*Translated from the Portuguese
by Margaret Jull Costa & Patricio Ferrari*

A NEW DIRECTIONS
PAPERBOOK ORIGINAL

 Book supported within the scope of the Open Call for Translation
of Literary Works by the Luso-American Development Foundation.

Manufactured in the United States of America
First published as New Directions Paperbook 1661 in 2026

Library of Congress Cataloging-in-Publication Data
Names: Pessoa, Fernando, 1888–1935 author | Pizarro, Jerónimo editor |
Uribe, Jorge editor | Costa, Margaret Jull translator | Ferrari, Patricio translator
Title: The complete works of Ricardo Reis / Fernando Pessoa ;
edited by Jerónimo Pizarro & Jorge Uribe ;
translated from the Portuguese by Margaret Jull Costa & Patricio Ferrari.
Identifiers: LCCN 2025049746 | ISBN 9780811237895 paperback |
ISBN 9780811237901 ebook
Subjects: LCSH: Reis, Ricardo, 1888–1935—Translations into English | LCGFT: Poetry
Classification: LCC PQ9261.P417 C64 2026
LC record available at https://lccn.loc.gov/20250497

10 9 8 7 6 5 4 3 2 1

New Directions Books are published for James Laughlin
by New Directions Publishing Corporation
80 Eighth Avenue, New York 10011

Contents

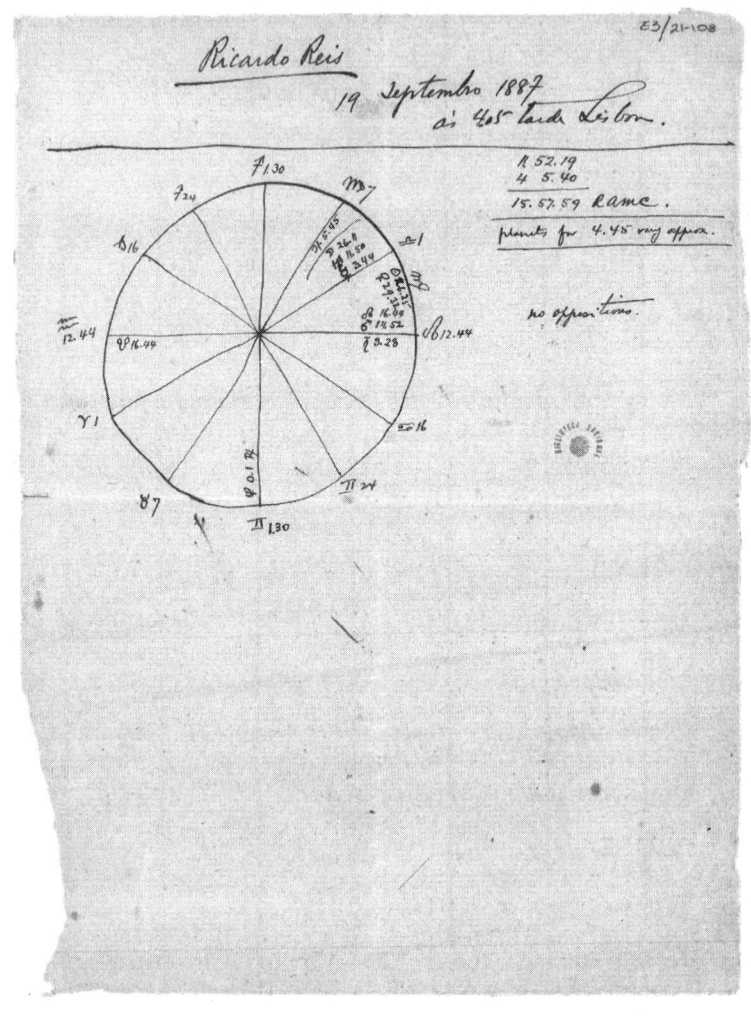

Horoscope for Ricardo Reis's date, time, and place of birth

A biographical note

Fernando Pessoa devoted his life to literature, producing an extraordinarily varied body of work that transcended dominant literary traditions or creeds—leaving to posterity two trunks filled to the brim with thousands upon thousands of unpublished writings. Born in Lisbon in 1888 and practically unknown outside of Portugal at the time of his death in 1935, he knew from an early age that his calling was the written word—exploring it across languages and genres while radically challenging the boundaries of authorship and subject. As a young boy he set out on his process of "self-othering" in English, a language he learned in the decade he spent in Durban, then under British rule, where his stepfather João Miguel Rosa (1857–1919) had been appointed Portuguese Consul. What Pessoa gained as an individual and in literary prowess during his formal education within the British Empire at the end of the Victorian era inexorably shaped his fate in Lisbon where he made his home for the remainder of his days.

That short yet prolific life may be divided neatly into three periods. In a letter to the *British Journal of Astrology* dated February 8, 1918, Pessoa wrote that there were only two dates he remembered with absolute precision: July 13, 1893, the date of his father's death from tuberculosis (when Pessoa was only five); and December 30, 1895, the day his mother remarried and, shortly after which, the family moved to South Africa. In that same letter, the twenty-nine-year-old Pessoa mentions a third date, too: August 20, 1905, the day he left South Africa and returned to Lisbon for good.

That first brief period was marked by two losses: the deaths of his father and of a younger brother. And perhaps a third loss too, that of his beloved Lisbon. During the second period, despite knowing only Portuguese when he arrived at the racially and ethnically diverse coastal city in eastern South Africa's KwaZulu-Natal Province, Pessoa rapidly became fluent in English and, to a lesser degree, in French. He was clearly no ordinary student. When asked years later, a fellow pupil described Pessoa in laudatory terms:

> [A]s a boy of 17 he wrote the article on Macaulay ... which I always regarded of exceptional merit. His English composition was generally remarkably good and sometimes approached to genius. He was a great admirer of Carlyle ... I was always very good friends with the boy and found him loyal and pub-lic-spirited. He was not athletic himself in ordinary English games; but I have been told by some of his contemporaries he was very easily excited after watching a game of football.[*]

In 1903, just seven years after arriving in Durban, Pessoa won first prize for an essay on the British historian Thomas Babington Macaulay. Indeed, he appeared to spend all his spare time among books, and had already started creating fictional alter egos—what he would later call heteronyms—for which he is now celebrated, writing poetry and prose under such names as Karl P. Effield, David Merrick, Charles Robert Anon, Horace James Faber, Alexander Search, and more. In a recent book, Jerónimo Pizarro and Patricio Ferrari introduced and anthologized nearly 140 fictional authors, some with their own specific biographies, literary influences, political views, and philosophical idiosyncrasies. Pessoa only articulated the concept of heteronymy toward the end of the 1920s.

> What Fernando Pessoa writes belongs to two categories of works, which we could call orthonymic works and hetero-nymic works. It is not possible to say that they are autonomous works and pseudonymous works because they are truly not.

[*] Quoted in Hubert D. Jennings. *The Poet with Many Faces: A Biography and Anthology*, ed. by Carlos Pittella (Providence: Gávea-Brown, 2018), p. 46.

Whereas the pseudonymous work is done by the author in his own person (the only difference being the name chosen for the signature), the heteronymic work is done by the author outside his personality. This is to say that it is the work of an individuality completely crafted by him as would be the sayings of characters in any of his dramas.*

The third period of Pessoa's life began when, at the age of seventeen, he returned alone to Lisbon, never to set foot on African soil again. He returned ostensibly to attend college, initially living with his maternal aunt and godmother, Anica, not far from the Curso Superior de Letras (the liberal arts faculty of the University of Lisbon). For different reasons—chief among them, ill health and a student strike—he abandoned his studies in 1907 and became a regular visitor to the National Library (which he had already begun frequenting during his second semester, in 1906, keeping a diary of his readings). There, he resumed his regime of voracious reading: philosophy, psychology, sociology, history, and, particularly, literature. During those first few years back in his native city, Pessoa reread his English masters (Shakespeare, Milton, Byron, Shelley, Keats), while also becoming acquainted with the works of Portuguese poets (Almeida Garrett, Antero de Quental, Cesário Verde, António Nobre, Guerra Junqueiro) and leading French symbolist poets (Baudelaire, Mallarmé, Verlaine), as well as the works of two American authors, Edgar Allan Poe and Walt Whitman, whose *Leaves of Grass* would have a great impact on his heteronymic work— primarily in Alberto Caeiro and Álvaro de Campos.†

Late in the summer of 1907, Dionísia Estrela de Seabra (1823–1907), Pessoa's paternal grandmother, left him a small legacy, and in the second half of 1909, he used that money to buy a printing press for

* Quoted from *Presença—Folha de Arte e Crítica* (Coimbra, n. 17, Dec. 1928), p. 10. The Portuguese magazine was published from 1927 until 1940.

† Alberto Caeiro is Pessoa's main poetic heteronym. Pessoa's other two major heteronyms, Ricardo Reis and Álvaro de Campos, and Pessoa himself considered Caeiro to be their literary master. While the first two wrote exclusively in Portuguese, Campos used English and French sparingly in his poetry. The three heteronyms emerged in 1914.

his publishing house, Empreza *Íbis*, which he set up a few months later. Empreza *Íbis* closed in 1910, having published not a single book. Needing to fend for himself, he turned to the one skill that most set him apart from his Portuguese contemporaries: foreign languages. Throughout the rest of his life, Pessoa would work as a freelance commercial translator (Portuguese, English, French) for various Lisbon-based import-export firms, never committing to the drudgery of a fixed schedule. Notably, it was around this time, in his early twenties, that the Portuguese (would-be English poet) finally embraced his mother tongue as his main literary language.

In 1912, he met the poet and fiction writer who would become his closest artistic ally and friend, Mário de Sá-Carneiro (1890–1916). That same year, Pessoa turned down an invitation from the American editor and publisher Warren F. Kellogg to work in London as a literary translator.[*] In April of 1912, Pessoa published his first piece of criticism in Portugal: a lengthy and provocative article entitled "The New Portuguese Poetry Sociologically Considered," in the review *A Águia* founded in Oporto two years earlier. From 1915 onward, Pessoa would continue contributing essays, as well as his own writings and translations, to various journals, including the literary magazine *Orpheu*, which he cofounded with artists and poets, among them Almada Negreiros (1893–1970) and Sá-Carneiro. Through this collaboration, he became part of Lisbon's literary avant-garde and was involved in various ephemeral literary movements such as Intersectionism and Sensationism. Alongside his day job, he wrote prolifically, producing poetry, fiction, and plays. Considering the massive number of writings that never made it into print during Pessoa's lifetime, it is fair to say that very little of his own poetry or prose was made available to his contemporaries—especially in England, where he managed to publish only one poem ("Meantime," in *The Athenaeum*, London, January 30, 1920).

At the end of the First World War, Pessoa printed two of the English

---

[*] Pessoa made his debut as a literary translator in the *Biblioteca Internacional de Obras Célebres* (1911–1912) with translations from English and Spanish.

works he had written during that decade: *Antinous*, a long poem that celebrates the homoerotic love between Antinous and the Emperor Hadrian, and *35 Sonnets*, inspired by Shakespeare's sonnet series. Both chapbooks were self-published in Lisbon in 1918. Three years later, in 1921, he self-published *English Poems I–II*, which included a revised version of "Antinous" and "Inscriptions," a series of epitaphs motivated by his reading of *The Greek Anthology*, translated into English by William Roger Paton. That same year, he also published *English Poems III* (*Epithalamium*), a sequence of twenty-one poems infused with explicit scenes of heterosexual love set in Rome. These two slim volumes were released by Olisipo, a commercial agency and publishing house that Pessoa had founded in 1921.

Literary fame came to Pessoa only posthumously. Besides these English chapbooks, which received some disparaging reviews, he managed to publish just one slender volume of forty-four poems in Portuguese—*Mensagem* (*Message*)—in December 1934, which secured him the recently established Antero de Quental Award. When Pessoa died in 1935, at the age of forty-seven, he left behind the famous trunks (there are at least two) stuffed with writings—nearly thirty thousand pieces of paper. Only then—thanks to some of his devoted literary friends and the many scholars who have since spent years excavating the archive—did he come to be recognized as the prolific genius he was.

Pessoa lived to write—writing, typing, or hastily scribbling on anything that came to hand: scraps of stationery, used envelopes, leaflets, advertising flyers, the backs of business letters, the flyleaves and margins of books in his personal library, dust jackets, tiny notebook sheets he would tear off and drop into the midst of his literary forest.

The creator of the heteronyms wrote voluminously—under his own name or another—in poetry, prose, drama, philosophy, criticism, and political theory—much of it unfinished or fragmentary. It is not unusual to find texts by different heteronyms on either side of a verso, commingling across the years. "All passes and remains," we read in the middle of loose sheets, between unfinished lines of an English poem titled "Elegy," which he probably wrote prior to the heteronymic eruption of 1914—a passage that, years later, will resonate with the closing line of Caeiro's penultimate poem in "The Keeper of Sheep": "Passo e fico, como o Universo" (I pass and I remain, like the universe).

All literary archived materials are dormant possibilities waiting to be awakened—as one rummages through a multilayered visual and acoustic space. This is the case with Pessoa's papers, where any reader may stumble upon his deep interest in esoterica: from occultism, theosophy, and astrology to Indian mysticism and Kabbalistic and Rosicrucian traditions. Yes, Pessoa drew up horoscopes not only for himself and his friends, but also for many dead writers and historical figures—among them Shakespeare, Wilde, and Robespierre—as well as for his heteronyms, a term he eventually chose over "pseudonym" because it more accurately described their stylistic and intellectual independence from him, their creator, and from each other. They sometimes interacted, even prefacing or criticizing each other's works.

Pessoa's most active early fictitious authors wrote primarily in English, leaving behind poetry in traditional verse forms such as the sonnet, rondeau, epigram, and epitaph, along with an astonishingly eclectic range of prose texts (philosophical notes, essays, short stories) mostly in the form of first drafts. Others—like the semi-heteronym Bernardo Soares, created around 1920 and associated with the posthumous *Book of Disquiet*, and his three main poetic heteronyms (Alberto Caeiro, Ricardo Reis, Álvaro de Campos)—produced a more substantial and cohesive body of work.

In an unfinished poem dated August 1, 1918—when Pessoa's focus was also on his English "Inscriptions—" we find what could be read as his own epitaph: "Genius, the greatest curse / That the Gods bless us with."[*] Pessoa wrote out of both necessity and conviction. May posterity judge his calling to the Gods.

PATRICIO FERRARI & MARGARET JULL COSTA

[*] Quoted in Patricio Ferrari, ed., *Inside the Mask: The English Poetry of Fernando Pessoa* (Providence: Gávea-Brown, 2018), p. 16.

Introduction

According to a letter Pessoa wrote to Adolfo Casais Monteiro early in 1935, less than a year before his death, Ricardo Reis "was born in 1887." He did not "remember the exact day and month, but this information must be somewhere among my papers."* In his detailed description, Pessoa says that Reis hailed from Oporto, describing him as "slightly, but only very slightly, shorter and sturdier [than Alberto Caeiro]." A doctor by profession with "a darkish complexion," he received his education at a Jesuit college, becoming a self-taught "Latinist" and "semi-Hellenist." In 1919, Reis left Portugal to live in voluntary exile in Brazil "because he was a monarchist." Born a year before Pessoa, Reis had a second birth in Pessoa's soul around 1912 when, in other documents, he made his first appearance, and a third, more substantial birth in 1914, when he emerged fully fledged and began writing his odes. In his letter, Pessoa implied that the appearance of Ricardo Reis coincided with that of Alberto Caeiro and of Álvaro de Campos—although Caeiro's writing emerged in March 1914, and that of Campos and Reis around June of the same year. But the most relevant aspect of Pessoa's fictitious account—that famous letter of January 13, 1935, quoted above—is not so much the precision of the dates, but the information it provides about Reis, who, at that time,

---

* Adolfo Casais Monteiro (1908–1972) was a Portuguese essayist, poet, and writer. Pessoa entrusted him with the most detailed account about the genesis of his heteronyms.

had already been living for at least twenty or so years in the soul from which he had emerged. The 1935 description is the last we have of Reis, and it confirms certain details, although just as Campos wasn't always described as being born in southern Portugal, in the coastal town of Tavira, Reis was not always presented as being a native of Oporto or physically exiled in South America.

In an earlier document, Reis is said to have been born in Lisbon—a poet of the Lisbon school, whose neoclassicism opposed the Maurrasian theories adopted in Portugal by Lusitanian Integralism; later, he continued to be a neoclassicist, born in Oporto, where the environment was more conducive to the project of restoring the monarchy.* The version that prevailed was the one Pessoa "fixed upon," so to speak, in the letter quoted above, but it is important to bear in mind that this fiction came very late and was part of a whole process. In the case of Reis, as with numerous other figures in Pessoa's expansive literary world, there are more questions than answers.

Was Reis always a monarchist? What kind of monarchism did he support? If we look at a 1914 text titled "Ricardo Reis—Life and Work," which is Pessoa's first attempt to offer a portrait of Reis, we discover, with surprise, that he was meant to "be born" on January 29, 1914, and to die on February 1, 1914; that is, Pessoa imagined an ephemeral Reis who would take on a single task: the development of "a 'scientific' neoclassicism ... in opposition to Maurrasian neoclassicism." This Reis initially would be a prose writer, an isolated figure without a master. Ricardo Reis may have studied medicine, since he is described as a doctor, but neither this nor his supposed monarchist tendencies is absolutely certain.

This curious 1914 text, which Pessoa abandoned in favor of presenting Reis as the author of a book of odes, shows that Reis, in terms of his life and works, grew in vitality and profundity, and that this growth was dependent on his becoming part of a dramatic ensemble.

* Charles Maurras (1868–1952) was a French nationalist, critic, and political theorist

A considerable part of Reis's writings consists of a dialogue with the works of Fernando Pessoa, Alberto Caeiro, Álvaro de Campos, and António Mora. Now, the fact that Reis's biography was constructed gradually raises similar questions, questions that the editors raised in *I Am An Anthology: 136 Fictional Authors*, a sort of Pessoa encyclopedia first published in Portugal in 2013:

> It is worth asking if Reis was always a Latinist or semi-Hellenist or if he only became so at a certain point. In our view, it is possible that these two attributes are also post-1914, or perhaps post-1916, when Reis received a commission to translate *Prometheus Bound* by Aeschylus, just as, in 1921, he was tasked with multiple translations of Sappho, Alcaeus, Aristotle, and some poems from the *Greek Anthology*. [*]

Ricardo Reis would, over time, have acquired and lost both attributes. Additionally, in 1914, Pessoa does not refer to Reis as a monarchist, and in 1935, he doesn't mention that Reis undertook certain translations (either because they were unfinished or because their authorship, assuming they were ever completed, was uncertain). This allows us to argue that the work generally preceded the biography. Specific historical events, such as the monarchist revolt of 1919, could also have influenced Reis's fictional biography. The Ricardian texts emerged not out of any one attribute—Reis being a doctor or a semi-Hellenist, for example—but out of the creative act itself. It is after the fact, and not at the moment of writing, that Pessoa places everything in what he called "moldes de realidade"—reality molds.

*

Neither the life nor the work of any of Pessoa's heteronyms was perfectly established at the time of his death in November 1935. Even Pessoa's own life remains shrouded in mystery. Very little of

---

[*] Fernando Pessoa, *Eu sou uma antologia: 136 autores fictícios*, ed. by Jerónimo Pizarro and Patricio Ferrari (Lisbon: Tinta-da-china, 2013), p. 421.

his work was published during his lifetime. In fact, his vast body of writing across genres and languages (Portuguese, English, French) is known primarily through successive and posthumous publications.

In the case of Reis's poetry, we found it necessary to define four core groups from a chronological perspective: (1) the book of odes projected in 1917 (odes written between 1914 and 1917); (2) the so-called "First Book," *Odes*, published in the magazine *Athena* (1924); (3) uncollected odes published in the magazine *Presença* between 1927 and 1933; (4) the "other odes and poems" (written over two decades, between 1914 and 1935) that remained unindexed or unpublished during Pessoa's lifetime.[*]

In the case of Reis's prose, we also identified three main groups: (1) the few texts intended as the preface to the book *Odes*; (2) the texts intended to introduce a book of poems by Alberto Caeiro; (3) texts on various subjects ranging from art to philosophy and religion. The prose texts in this volume, like those in the previous New Directions volumes, are arranged chronologically.

The editorial challenges remain the same over the years: refining the readings of handwritten texts (Pessoa's calligraphy is not always easy to decipher), reading the entirety of Pessoa's output (approximately 30,000 documents), defining what belongs or could belong to certain fictional authors, organizing each textual corpus clearly, and proposing well-informed critical dates. In the case of Ricardo Reis, some transcriptions have been refined over decades; some poems took time to enter the Ricardian canon because they were (and are) published as texts by Fernando Pessoa.[†] Some prose texts were first attributed to António Mora (by Luís Filipe Bragança Teixeira)

---

[*] *Athena* was a monthly art magazine, launched in Lisbon in October 1924; five issues were published, under the literary direction of Fernando Pessoa and the artistic direction of Ruy Vaz. *Presença: Folha de Arte e Crítica* was a Portuguese magazine published in Coimbra from March 10, 1927, until 1940, with a total of fifty-four issues.

[†] See the Imprensa Nacional–Casa da Moeda (INCM) critical edition of Pessoa's works, edited by Ivo Castro.

and then to Reis (by Manuela Parreira da Silva). To read Reis in this *Complete Works*, based on the Tinta-da-china edition and now in English for the first time, is to read a more accurately deciphered, more complete, and more diachronic Reis.

*

If Caeiro's triumphal day was March 8, 1914, Reis's was June 12, 1914, the eve of Fernando Pessoa's twenty-sixth birthday. Pessoa, as Reis, wrote at least six odes, and in that month, a total of approximately fifteen. This burst of productivity prompted Pessoa to tell his close friend and fellow poet Mário de Sá-Carneiro about Reis, and, on June 23, 1914, Sá-Carneiro sent Pessoa his "sincere congratulations on the birth of Sr. Ricardo Reis"—saying he was "eager" to read all the odes.* On June 27, again from Paris, where Sá-Carneiro was living and where, two years later, he would commit suicide, he praised the novelty of these "works," picking out several odes for special mention:

> The odes of Ricardo Reis are admirable, my dear Poet. He has created something "novel" in the classical, Horatian tradition. For that is the impression they left me with. I'm not sure why, for while they contain new elements, they are nevertheless classical, pagan. And if I may say so: the poems are a marvel of impersonality, for if Master Fernando Pessoa was still evident in Caeiro, this is not the case in Reis's poems. They—being Yours in beauty and in Genius—are very much his. The first stanza of the first ode is something very great, very new—in its simplicity and its classicism. Could we describe little Ricardo Reis as a Horace multiplied by soul? Reading through the other odes, I found admirable things at every step.†

---

* See Mário de Sá-Carneiro, *Em ouro e alma: Correspondência com Fernando Pessoa*, ed. Ricardo Vasconcelos and Jerónimo Pizarro (Lisbon, Tinta-da-china, 2015), p. 211.

† See Sá-Carneiro (2015), p. 218

In 1914 alone, Pessoa wrote at least forty odes, thirty-six of which were listed in an initial book plan under the heading *Odes*. A second grouping, dating from 1917, contains forty-one odes, while later plans from 1923–1924 contain only twenty odes—the ones he eventually published in *Athena*. Pessoa did not stop writing odes before or after introducing Reis in this magazine.

The odes published in the inaugural issue of *Athena*, in 1924, form a "First Book" (Odes 42 to 61), which critic and editor Silva Belkior describes as "an organic whole, a cohesive unit, created by Fernando Pessoa," as well as being thematically organized. Belkior writes: "In this selection we find a group of twenty odes: sixteen on the brevity of life; one on the great dead poet, an unparalleled master; one on the farmer, a model of a tranquil and happy existence; and two on the art of poetry. Thus, the 'First Book' is a kind of expansive poem, divided into twenty small odes."* This "expansive poem" dialogues with Horatian models from the very first lines. "Seated securely on the solid pillar / Of the verses in which I remain" (Ode 42) imitates the beginning of the last ode of Horace's Book III, "Exegi monumentum aere perennius / Regalique situ pyramidum altius" [I erected a monument more lasting than bronze / In a royal site higher than pyramids], as observed by critic Maria Helena da Rocha Pereira.† But Reis isn't merely a new Horace; he is a "Greek Horace who writes in Portuguese," as Pessoa tells us in a note datable to 1916–1917, a poet with growing autonomy, subtly refining a few classical influences.

Regarding the set of odes published in *Presença*, eight in total, Belkior notes their lack of cohesion, stating that "the Poet [Pessoa] was not interested in themes here, but in the rhythm of the dates of composition." Belkior highlights that "this collection lacks any reference to a 'book,'" that "in submitting these small, perfectly formed

* See Silva Belkior, *Fernando Pessoa/Ricardo Reis: os originais* (Lisbon, Imprensa Nacional–Casa da Moeda, 1983), pp. 51–52.

† See "Reflexos horacianos nas odes de Correia Garção e Fernando Pessoa/Ricardo Reis)." *Temas Clássicos na Poesia Portuguesa* (Lisbon/São Paulo, Verbo, 2008), pp. 77–78.

poems for publication, the Poet was merely responding to persistent requests for contributions."* We have grouped together these eight odes to help make a clearer distinction between what was published during Pessoa's lifetime and what was not, and to explore different phases of Ricardo Reis's output.

This is Reis the poet. But there is also Reis the prose writer, whose work appears in the second part of this volume. Reis the prose writer became better known with the publication in Portugal of *Páginas Íntimas e de Auto-Interpretação* (Personal pages and self-reflection) in 1966 by editors Georg Rudolf Lind and Jacinto do Prado Coelho. According to Pessoa, in a text dated from 1931, it is poetry that predominates in the writings of the heteronyms, because "in prose it is more difficult to 'other' oneself."† In that letter of 13 January 1935 mentioned earlier, Pessoa says:

> Reis [writes] better than I do, but with a purism I consider exaggerated. The difficult thing for me is to write Reis's prose— still unpublished—or Campos's. Simulation is easier in poetry, perhaps because it is more spontaneous.

Reis's prose must have cost Pessoa "a terrible effort of impersonation" and was published only posthumously. Much like Álvaro de Campos's prose, it's most interesting aspect is that it dialogues with his poetic output as well as with the other works within Pessoa's literary universe.

*

The Complete Works of Ricardo Reis gathers together all the texts considered attributable to Ricardo Reis—acknowledging that the debate about what can or cannot be attributed to Reis will always

---

* See Belkior, pp. 54–55.
† See Fernando Pessoa, *Livro do Desasocego* (*The Book of Disquiet*), ed. by Jerónimo Pizarro. Lisbon (Imprensa Nacional–Casa da Moeda, 2 vols, 2010, volume 1), p. 457.

remain open. As with the prose section in the Alberto Caeiro and Álvaro de Campos volumes published by New Directions, only a selection of Reis's prose texts is included. The rest can be found on the New Directions website and in *Pessoa Plural*, an international peer-reviewed scholarly journal dedicated to the study of Fernando Pessoa, established in 2012.

This volume, like the others, was translated by Margaret Jull Costa and Patricio Ferrari. It completes a trilogy featuring the works of Pessoa's three main heteronyms. It aims to deepen our understanding of Pessoa's coterie, or the "family discussion" project, as it is described in a list datable to 1932.[*] Each volume can be read independently but also forms an integral part of a larger set.

In his later years, Pessoa, who always playfully claimed to have "nothing to do with the matter" and to be "the least important member," was preparing to publish the work of the heteronyms, and frequently mentioned the aesthetic discussion between Reis and Campos in his letters. Today, we can read these "Fictions of the Interlude" and finally understand why Pessoa is the most universal author in the Portuguese language and one of the most representative writers of Modernism.

*

This volume is based on the first complete critical edition of Ricardo Reis's writings, published by Tinta-da-china in Portugal (2016). That Portuguese edition preserves original spellings and includes all textual variants found in Pessoa's manuscripts and typescripts, while also correcting and refining earlier transcriptions by previous editors. Since the New Directions edition is not a critical one, it does not include variant readings beyond the final ones. The only other omissions here are the texts gathered in the Annexes—namely,

---

[*] See Fernando Pessoa, *Obra Completa de Álvaro de Campos* (*Complete Works of Álvaro de Campos*), ed. by Jerónimo Pizarro, Antonio Cardiello, Jorge Uribe, Filipa Freitas (Lisbon: Tinta-da-china, 2014), p. 575.

certain incomplete odes left unattributed by Pessoa, as well as prose texts also unatrributed and either fragmentary or unfinished drafts. This edition features numerous poems and prose texts never before translated into English, also with selected facsimiles from the Pessoa Archive at the National Library of Portugal in Lisbon.

JERÓNIMO PIZARRO

Acknowledgments

The editors are grateful to Pedro Serpa, Vera Tavares, Rita Almeida Simões, Rute Diaz Paiva, Catarina Homem Marques, and Bárbara Bulhosa at Tinta-da-china, where the Fernando Pessoa Collection, established and directed by Jerónimo Pizarro, continues to flourish and expand.

The translators wish to acknowledge the publications where the following texts first appeared:

Ode 1, in *The New Yorker* (ed. Kevin Young), (2026).

Odes 9, 11, 112, 218, and 219, in *Poetry* (ed. Adrian Matejka), Volume 227, no. 4 (Jan./Feb, 2026), with a translators' note on the magazine's blog.

Odes 42/1 and 163, in *The New York Review of Books* (ed. Jana Prikryl), (Spring 2026)

Odes 66 and 143, in *Southwest Review* (ed. Greg Brownderville), Volume 111, No. 1 (Spring 2026)

Ode 76, in *The Paris Review* (ed. Srikanth Reddy), Issue No. 252 (Summer 2025).

Ode 86, in *The Threepenny Review* (ed. Wendy Lesser), Issue 185 (Spring 2026)

The editors and translators extend their heartfelt thanks to Barbara Epler and Declan Spring at New Directions for warmly welcoming the works of Fernando Pessoa into their literary home. We are especially grateful to Declan Spring for his meticulous editorial work on each of the Pessoa volumes and to Maya Solovej for her thoughtful management of the project's publicity. Our appreciation also goes to the entire New Directions team for their professionalism, diligence, and steadfast commitment to modern US and world literature.

Poems

Odes (1914–1917)

1

Mestre, são plácidas
Todas as horas
Que nós perdemos,
Se no perdel-as,
Qual n'uma jarra,
Nós pômos flores.

Não ha tristezas
Nem alegrias
Na nossa vida.
Assim saibamos,
Sabios incautos,
Não a viver,

Mas decorrel-a,
Tranquillos, placidos,
Tendo as creanças
Por nossas mestras,
E os olhos cheios
De Natureza...

Á beira-rio,
Á beira-estrada,
Conforme calha,
Sempre no mesmo
Leve descanço
De estar vivendo.

O tempo passa,
Não nos diz nada.
Envelhecemos.
Saibamos, quasi
Maliciosos,
Sentir-nos ir.

2

1

Master, how serene
Are all the hours
We waste
If, as we waste them,
We place them in a vase
Like flowers.

There are no sorrows
In our lives
Nor joys either.
Let us learn, then,
Innocent sages,
Not to live life

But to pass through it,
Tranquil, serene,
Taking children
As our teachers,
Eyes full
Of Nature …

Beside a river,
Beside a road,
Wherever we are,
Living life
With the same
Light ease.

Time passes,
And tells us nothing.
We grow old.
Let us learn, almost
Mischievously,
To feel ourselves leaving.

Não vale a pena
Fazer um gesto.
Não se resiste
Ao deus atroz
Que os proprios filhos
Devora sempre.

Colhamos flores.
Molhemos leves
As nossas mãos
Nos rios calmos,
Para aprendermos
Calma tambem.

Girasoes sempre
Fitando o sol,
Da vida iremos
Tranquillos, tendo
Nem o remorso
De ter vivido.

2
Da lampada nocturna
A chamma estremece
E o quarto alto ondeia.

Os deuses concedem
Aos seus calmos crentes
Que nunca lhes trema
A chamma da vida
Perturbando o aspecto
Do que está em roda,
Mas firme e esguiada

There is no point
In doing anything,
There is no resisting
The monstrous god
Who devours
His own children.

Let us gather flowers.
Let us bathe our hands
In the calm rivers,
And from them
Learn their calm.

Sunflowers eternally
Staring at the sun,
We will leave life
Tranquilly, not even
Regretting
Having lived.

2   [2 August 1914]
The nightlight flickers
And the high-ceilinged
Room quivers.

The gods promise
Their calm believers
That the flame of life
Will never tremble,
Troubling the surface
Of everything around,
But stand firm, erect

Como preciosa
E antiga pedra,
Guarde a sua calma
Beleza continua.

3

Este, seu escasso campo ora lavrando,
Ora, cançado, olhando-o com a vista
    De quem a um filho olha
    Passa alegre na vida.

Pouco lhe importa sob que Deus arrasta
A obra, louvores doutos ou nescios
    São lhe a mesma distancia
    De todos os seus dias ...

Figura eterna longe das cidades,
Passa na vida sob a maior graça
    Que os deuses nos concedem—
    Que é não se nos mostrarem

Nas activas presenças encobertos
Com o ceu e a terra e o riso das seáras
    Quaes ricos disfarçados
    Dando aos pobres sem gloria ...

4

Não tenhas nada nas mãos
Nem uma memoria na alma,

Que quando te puzerem
Nas mãos o óbolo ultimo,

Like some precious
Ancient stone,
Maintaining its calm,
Unchanging beauty.

3   [27 September 1914]
This man, working his scant field,
Or, grown weary, pausing to gaze
        Like a father at his son,
        Lives life contentedly.

He cares little about the God he labors under,
And praise, whether learnèd or foolish,
        Is as indifferent to him
        As are all his days ...

An eternal figure far from cities,
He passes through life with the greatest blessing
        The gods deign to grant us—
        Namely, not to reveal themselves to us

Concealed within the active presences
Of sky and land and the laughter of wheatfields,
        Like rich men in disguise, who,
        Quite unsung, give alms to the poor ...

4   [19 June 1914]
Hold nothing in your hands,
Nor a single memory in your soul,

So that when the final obol
Is placed in your hands,

Ao abrirem-te as mãos
Nada te cahirá.

Que throno te querem dar
Que Atropos t'o não tire?

Que louros que não fanem
Nos arbitrios de Minos?

Que horas que te não tornem
Da estatura da sombra

Que serás quando fôres
Na noite e ao fim da estrada?

Colhe as flores mas larga-as,
Das mãos mal as olhaste.

Senta-te ao sol. Abdica
E sê rei de ti proprio.

5
Quero, Neëra, que os teus labios laves
    Na nascente tranquilla
Para que contra a tua febre e a triste
    Dor que pões em viver,
Sintas a fresca e calma natureza
    Da agua, e reconheças
Que não têm penas nem desasocegos
    As nymphas das nascentes
Nem mais soluços do que o som da agua
    Alegre e natural.
       —

And you open them to receive it,
Nothing else will fall from them.

What throne can you be given
That Atropos will not take from you?

What laurels will not wither
Upon a decree from King Minos?

What hours will not reduce you
To the stature of the shadow

You will be when you set off
Into the night at the end of the road?

Yes, pick flowers, but discard them
Once you have looked at them.

Sit down in the sun. Abdicate,
And be king of yourself.

5 [c. 11 July 1914]

Neaira, I want you to moisten your lips
    In the tranquil spring water
So that you quell the fever and pain
    Of living your life
With the water's cool, calm nature
    And come to realize
That the nymphs of the springs
    Know no sorrows, no disquiets,
And, as for tears, know only the happy, natural
    Sound of the water.

        —

As nossas dores, não, Neëra, veem
Das causas naturaes
Datam da alma e do infeliz fruir
Da vida com os homens.
Aprende pois, ó aprendiza jovem
Das classicas delicias,
A não pôr mais tristeza que um suspiro
No modo como vives.
Nasceste pallida, deitando a agua
Da tua vã belleza
Sobr a estiolada fé das nossas mãos
Medrosas de ter goso
Demasiado preso á desconfiança
Que vem de teu saber,
Não para essa vã mnemonica
Do futuro fatal.
Façamos vividas grinaldas varias
De sol, flores e risos
Para occultar o fundo fiel á Noite
Do nosso pensamento
Curvado já em vida sob a idéa
Do plutonico jugo
Conscia já da livida aguardança
Do chaos redivivo.

6
Ao longe os montes teem neve ao sol,
Mas é suave já o frio calmo
Que alisa e agudece
Os dardos do sol alto.

Hoje, Neëra, não nos escondamos,
Nada nos falta, porque nada somos.

10

Our griefs, Neaira, do not come
    From natural causes,
But from the soul and the misfortune
    Of having to live among men.
Learn, then, my young apprentice,
    From the classical delights,
And invest no more sadness than a sigh
    In the way that you live.
You were born pale, pouring the water
    Of your futile beauty
On the etiolated faith of our hands,
    So fearful of feeling a pleasure
Too closely allied with the distrust
    Born of your experience,
Rather than that vain mnemonic
    Of our fateful future.
Let us weave brightly colored garlands
    Made of sun and flowers and laughter
To conceal the nagging thought,
    Still faithful to the Night,
Already bent beneath the idea
    Of the Plutonic yoke,
And already aware of the pallid prospect
    Of chaos reborn.

6   [16 June 1914]

There's sunlight on the distant snowy hills,
But it's milder now, and the calm cold
    Hones and sharpens
    The darts of midday sun.

Today, Neaira, we need not hide,
For, being nothing, we lack for nothing.

Não esperamos nada
E temos frio ao sol.

Mas tal como é, gosemos o momento,
Solemnes na alegria levemente,
    E aguardando a morte
    Como quem a conhece.

7

O deus Pan não morreu,
Cada campo que mostra
Aos sorrisos de Apollo
Os peitos nus de Ceres—
Cedo ou tarde vereis
Por lá aparecer
O deus Pan, o immortal.

Não matou outros deuses
O triste deus christão.
Christo é um deus a mais,
Talvez um que faltava.
Pan continúa a dar
Os sons da sua flauta
Aos ouvidos de Ceres
Recumbente nos campos.

Os deuses são os mesmos,
Sempre claros e calmos,
Cheios de eternidade
E desprezo por nós,
Trazendo o dia e a noite
E as colheitas douradas
Sem ser para nos dar

Expect nothing,
And shiver in the sun.

But let us enjoy the moment, such as it is,
Feeling slightly solemn in our happiness,
    While we wait for death
    As if we had met it before.

7   [12 June 1914]

The god Pan is not dead.
In every field that reveals
To Apollo's smiles
The bare breasts of Ceres—
Sooner or later, you will see
Appear there
The god Pan, the immortal one.

The sad Christian god
Did not kill the other gods.
Christ is just another god,
Perhaps one that was missing.
Pan continues to send
The sounds of his flute
To the ears of Ceres
Where she lies in the fields.

The gods are the same gods,
Always clear and calm,
Full of eternity
And scorn for us,
Bringing day and night
And the golden harvests
Not in order to give us

13

O dia e a noite e o trigo
Mas por outro e divino
Proposito casual.

8

De Apollo o carro rodou pra fóra
Da vista. A poeira que levantára
Ficou enchendo de leve névoa
        O horisonte…

A flauta calma de Pan, descendo
Seu tom agudo no ar pausado,
Deu mais tristezas ao moribundo
        Dia suave.

Cálida e loura, nubil e triste,
Tu, mondadeira dos prados quentes,
Ficas ouvindo, com os teus passos
        Mais arrastados,

A flauta antiga do deus durando
Com o ar que cresce pra vento leve,
E sei que pensas na deusa clara
        Nada dos mares,

E que vão ondas lá muito adentro
Do que o teu seio sente alheado
De quanto a flauta sorrindo chora
        E estás ouvindo.

Day and night and wheat
But for some other divine
And arbitrary purpose.

8 [12 June 1914]

Apollo's chariot rolled out
Of sight. The dust it raised
Filled the horizon with
      a light mist …

Pan's calm flute, laying
Its high notes on the slow air,
Lent more sadnesses to the sweet
      Dying day.

Warm and fair, nubile and sad,
You, weeder of parched fields,
Are listening, your steps growing
      Ever wearier,

To the god's ancient flute that lingers
On the air that is now becoming a breeze,
And I know you're thinking of the bright goddess
      Born of the seas,

That, deep inside, waves are breaking,
That your heart, however, is elsewhere,
While the flute smilingly weeps
      And you listen.

9

Sabio é o que se contenta com o espectaculo do mundo,
    E ao beber nem recorda
    Que já bebeu na vida,
    Para quem tudo é novo
    E immarcessivel sempre.

Corôem-o pampanos, ou heras, ou rosas voluteis,
    Elle sabe que a vida
    Passa por ele e tanto
    Corta á flôr como a elle
    De Atropos a thesoura.

Mas elle sabe fazer que a côr do vinho esconda isto,
    Que o seu sabôr orgiaco
    Apague o gosto ás horas,
    Como a uma voz chorando
    O passar das bacchantes.

E elle espera, contente quasi e bebedor tranquilo,
    E apenas desejando
    N'um desejo mal tido
    Que a abominavel onda
    O não molhe tão cedo.

10

Os deuses desterrados,
Os irmãos de Saturno,
Ás vezes, no crepusculo
Vêm espreitar a vida.*

* Note that different spellings (vêem and vem) coexist in the Portuguese text.

9

Wise is the man contented with the mere spectacle of the world,
    Who, when he drinks, has no memory
    Of ever having drunk before,
    For whom all is new
    And for ever imperishable.

Crown him with vines or ivy or with twining roses,
    He knows that life passes
    By him and through him
    And that both he and the flower
    Will fall to Atropos's scissors.

He knows, though, how to conceal this fact with red wine,
    And uses its orgiastic savor
    To blunt the taste of the passing hours,
    Like a voice grieving for
    The passing of the bacchantes.

And he waits, this tranquil drinker, feeling almost content,
    With just one wish,
    If indeed it is a wish,
    That it does not break over him
    Too soon, that odious wave.

10

Sometimes, at twilight,
The exiled gods,
Saturn's brothers,
Come to take a look at life.

Vem então ter comnosco
Remorsos e saudades
E sentimentos falsos.
É a presença d'elles,
Deuses que o desthronal-os
Tornou espirituaes,
De materia vencida,
Longinqua e inactiva.

Vêem, inuteis forças,
Solicitar em nós
As dores e os cansaços,
Que nos tiram da mão,
Como a um bebado molle,
A taça da alegria.

Vêem fazer-nos crêr,
Despeitadas ruinas
De primitivas forças,
Que o mundo é mais extenso
Que o que se vê e palpa,
Para que offendamos
A Jupiter e a Apollo.

Assim até á beira
Terrena do horisonte
Hyperion no crepusculo
Vem chorar pelo carro
Que Apollo lhe roubou.

E o poente tem côres
Da dôr d'um deus longinquo,

They come to share with us
Remorse and longing
And other such false feelings.
Thus they make their presence felt,
Gods who, once dethroned,
Became purely spiritual,
Made of vanquished matter,
Remote, inactive.

They come, those futile forces,
To provoke in us
Sorrows and tediums,
To snatch from our hand,
As if from some flaccid drunk,
The cup of happiness.

They come to convince us,
Those resentful ruins
Of once-potent forces,
That the world is larger
Than anything we see and touch,
And so have us offend
Against Jupiter and Apollo.

So it is, at twilight,
On the horizon's earthly shore,
That Hyperion arrives
To mourn the chariot
Apollo stole from him.

And the sunset wears the colors
Of the grief of a distant god,

E ouve-se soluçar
Para além das espheras ...

Assim choram os deuses.

11
Coroae-me de rosas
Coroae-me em verdade
     De rosas.

Quero ter a hora
Nas mãos pagãmente
     E leve,

Mal sentir a vida,
Mal sentir o sol
     Sob ramos.

Coroae-me de rosas
E de folhas de hera
     E basta.

12
Vem sentar-te commigo, Lydia, á beira do rio.
Socegadamente fitemos o seu curso e aprendamos
Que a vida passa, e não estamos de mãos enlaçadas.
     (Enlacemos as mãos).

Depois pensemos, creanças adultas, que a vida
Passa e não fica, nada deixa e nunca regressa,
Vae para um mar muito longe, para ao pé do Fado,
     Mais longe que os deuses.

Who can be heard sobbing
Somewhere beyond the spheres ...

This is how the gods weep.

11

Crown me with roses
Yes, really, crown me
    With roses.

I want to hold the hour
In my hands paganly,
    Lightly,

Barely feeling life,
Barely feeling the sun
    Beneath the branches.

Crown me with roses
And with ivy leaves,
    Nothing more.

12   [12 June 1914]

Come and sit with me, Lydia, beside the river.
Let us quietly watch it flowing past and learn
That life, too, passes, and that we are not holding hands.
    (Let us hold hands.)

Then let us think, like grown-up children, that life
Passes and doesn't stay, leaves nothing behind and never returns,
It flows down to a far-distant sea, close to Fate itself,
    Even farther off than the gods.

Desenlacemos as mãos, porque não vale a pena cançarmo-nos.
Quer gosemos, quer não gosemos, passamos como o rio.
Mais vale saber passar silenciosamente
	E sem desassocegos grandes.

Sem amores, nem odios, nem paixões que levantam a voz,
Nem invejas que dão movimento de mais aos olhos,
Nem cuidados, porque se os tivesse o rio sempre correria,
	E sempre iria ter ao mar.

Amêmo-nos tranquillamente, pensando que podiamos,
Se quizessemos, trocar beijos e abraços e caricias,
Mas que mais vale estarmos sentados ao pé um do outro
	Ouvindo correr o rio e vendo-o.

Colhamos flores, pega tu n'ellas e deixa-as
No collo, e que o seu perfume suavize o momento—
Este momento em que socegadamente não cremos em nada,
	Pagãos innocentes da decadencia.

Ao menos, se fôr sombra antes, lembrar-te-has de mim depois
Sem que a minha lembrança te arda ou te fira ou te mova,
Porque nunca enlaçamos as mãos, nem nos beijamos
	Nem fômos mais do que creanças.

E se antes do que eu levares o óbolo ao barqueiro sombrio,
Eu nada terei que soffrer ao lembrar-me de ti.
Ser-me-has suave á memoria lembrando-te assim—á beira-rio,
	Pagã triste e com flores no regaço.

Let us stop holding hands, why weary ourselves.
Whether we like it or not, we pass like the river.
Better then to learn to pass silently,
    With no major disquiets.

With no loves, no hatreds, or loud passions raising their voices,
No envious feelings making our eyes shift restlessly about,
No cares, because even if we had them, the river would still run,
    And still flow down to the sea.

Let us love each other tranquilly, thinking that we could,
If we wished, exchange kisses, embraces, and caresses,
But how much better it is to sit here side by side
    Listening to and watching the river flow past.

Let us pick flowers, yes, pick some flowers and place them
In your lap, and let their perfume sweeten the moment—
This moment when we quietly believe in nothing at all,
    Innocent pagans of a decadent age.

At least, if I am the first to become a shadow, you'll remember me
    later
Without that memory tormenting or wounding or moving you,
Because we never did hold hands, nor did we kiss,
    Nor were we ever more than children.

And if you are the first to hand the obol to the grim boatman,
I will have no reason to suffer when I remember you.
You'll be a balm to my memory when I think of you like this—
    beside the river,
    A sad pagan maid with flowers in her lap.

13

Breve o inverno virá com sua branca
    Nudez vestir os campos.
As lareiras serão as nossas patrias
    E os contos que contarmos
Assentados ao pé do seu calôr
    Valerão as canções
Com que outr'ora entre as verdes hervas rijas
    Diziamos ao sol
O ave atque vale triste e alegre,
    Solemnes e carpindo.
Porora o outomno está comnosco ainda.
    Se elle nos não agrada
A memoria do estio cotejemos
    Com a esp'rança hiemal.
E entre essas dadivas memoradas
    Como esse rio passemos.

14

Aqui, Neera, longe
De homens e de cidades,
Por ninguem nos tolher
O passo, nem vedarem
A nossa vista as casas,
Podemos crer-nos livres.

Bem sei, ó flava, que inda
Nos tolhe a vida o corpo,
E não temos a mão
Onde temos o gosto;
Bem sei que mesmo aqui
Se nos gasta esta carne

24

13

Soon winter will come to clothe the fields
    With its white nakedness.
The fireside will be our homeland
    And the stories we tell
As we sit enjoying its warmth
    Will be like the songs
That, once, among the lush green grasses,
    We sang to the sun,
The sad and joyful ave atque vale,
    Solemn and mournful.
For the moment, though, autumn is still with us.
    And if that does not please us,
Let us compare our memory of summer
    With our hibernal hopes.
And among those remembered gifts
    Let us pass like that river.

14

Here, Neaira, far
From men and cities,
With no one to hamper
Our steps, with no houses
To block our view,
We can believe we are free.

I know, O golden one, that
Our body still hampers our life,
And our hand is not
Where our heart is;
I know that even here
This flesh is growing old,

Que os deuses concederam
Ao estado antes de Averno.

Mas aqui não nos prendem
Mais coisas do que a vida,
Mãos alheias não tomam
Do nosso braço, ou passos
Humanos se atravessam
Pelo nosso caminho.

Se a nossa vida esquece
Poderemos julgarmo-nos
Livres inteiramente.
Por isso não pensemos
E deixemo-nos crer
Na inteira liberdade
E essa illusão de agora
Far-nos-ha como os deuses.

15

A pallidez do dia é levemente dourada.
O sol de inverno faz luzir como orvalho as curvas
    Dos troncos e ramos seccos.
    O frio leve treme.

Desterrado da patria antiquissima da minha
Crença, consolado só por pensar nos deuses
    Aqueço-me tremulo
    A outro sol do que este.

O sol que havia sobre o Parthenon e a Acropole
O que alumiava os passos lentos e graves
    De Aristoteles fallando.
    Mas Epicuro melhor

A flesh granted us by the gods
In our pre-Avernus state.

But here we are not held
By anything other than life,
No hands reach out to take
Our arm, no human steps
Cross our path.

If we could only forget our life,
Then we could deem ourselves
To be entirely free.
So let us stop thinking
And let us believe
In that total freedom,
And that momentary illusion
Will make us as gods.

15   [19 June 1914]
The paleness of day is slightly gilded.
The winter sun makes the curved tree trunks
        And bare branches glitter like dew.
        The light cold shivers.

Exiled from the very ancient homeland of my
Belief, with the memory of the gods my only consolation,
        And, shivering, I warm myself
        On another sun than this one.

The sun that shone on the Parthenon and the Acropolis,
The same sun that lit the slow, grave steps
        Of Aristotle as he spoke.
        Although Epicurus speaks

Me falla, com a sua cariciosa voz terrestre
Tendo para os deuses uma atitude tambem de deus,
    Sereno e vendo a vida
    Á distancia a que está.

16

De anjos ou deuses, sempre nós tivemos,
A visão confiada de que acima
    De nós e compellindo-nos
    Agem outras presenças.

Como acima dos gados que ha nos campos
O nosso esforço, que eles não comprehendem,
    Os coage e obriga
    E eles não nos percebem.

Nossa vontade e o nosso pensamento
São as mãos pelas quaes outros nos guiam
    Para onde elles querem
    Que nós o desejemos.

17

Da nossa semelhança com os deuses
    Por nosso bem tiremos
Julgarmo-nos deidades exiladas
    E possuindo a Vida
Por uma autoridade primitiva
    E coëva de Jove.

Altivamente donos de nós-mesmos,
    Usemos a existencia
Como a villa que os deuses nos concedem
    Para esquecer o estio.

To me more clearly, with his caressing, earthly voice,
Treating the gods as a god would treat them,
        Serenely, and seeing life
        As the distant thing it is.

16   [16 October 1914]

Be they angels or gods, we have always had
The certain notion that above us,
        Driving us along,
        Are other presences.

Just as we, over the cattle in the fields,
Impose our will on their uncomprehending selves,
        To coerce and oblige them,
        Without their even noticing,

So our will and our thoughts
Are the hands by which others lead us
        Wherever they want
        Us to choose to go.

17   [30 July 1914]

Regarding our resemblance to the gods,
        Let us, for our own good,
Believe ourselves to be exiled deities
        Who were granted Life
By a more primitive authority
        Coeval with Jove.

Proud masters of ourselves,
        Let us use existence
Like the villa lent us by the gods
        To forget the summer.

Não de outra forma mais apoquentada
    Nos vale o esforço usarmos
A existencia indecisa e afluente
    Fatal do rio escuro.

Como acima dos deuses o Destino
    É calmo e inexoravel,
Acima de nós-mesmos construamos
    Um fado voluntario
Que quando nos opprima nós sejamos
    Esse que nos oprime,
E quando entremos pela noite dentro
    Por nosso pé entremos.

18

Cuidas tu, louro Flacco, que apertando
Teus infecundos, trabalhosos dias
    Em feixes de hirta lenha,
    Cumpres a tua vida?

A tua lenha é só peso que levas
Para onde não tens fogo que te aqueça,
    Nem levam peso aos hombros
    As sombras que seremos.

Aprende calma com o ceu unido
E com a fonte a ter continuo curso.
    Não sejas a clepsydra
    Que conta a hora de outros.

Why resort to more effortful ways
        Of making use of
This indecisive existence, this fatal
        Tributary of the dark river?

Like the Destiny that hovers over the gods,
        Calm and inexorable,
Let us build for ourselves
        Our own self-imposed fate,
So that when we feel oppressed,
        We are our own oppressors,
And when we enter that dark night,
        we enter of our own free will.

18   [11 July 1914]

Do you really think, fair Flaccus, that in binding
Your fruitless, wearisome days
        Into bundles of stiff firewood,
        You are really living your life?

Your firewood is merely the weight you carry
To a place where no fire will warm you.
        Besides, the shadows we will become
        Carry no great weight on their shoulders.

Learn serenity from the vaulted sky
And, from the spring, learn simply to flow.
        Do not be like the water clock
        Counting the hours of others.

19

O mar jaz. Gemem em segredo os ventos
    Em eolo captivos,
Apenas com as pontas do tridente
    Franze as aguas Neptuno,
E a praia é alva e cheia de pequenos
    Brilhos sob o sol claro.
Eu quizera, Neera, que o momento,
    Que ora vemos, tivesse
O sentido preciso de uma phrase
    Visivel n'algum livro.
Assim verias que certeza a minha
    Quando sem te olhar digo
Que as cousas são o dialogo que os deuses
    Brincam tendo comnosco.
Se esta breve sciencia te coubesse,
    Nunca mais julgarias
Ou solemne ou ligeira a clara vida,
    Mas nem leve nem grave,
Nem falsa ou certa, mas assim, divina
    E placida, e mais nada.

20

Neëra, passeemos junctos
Só para nos lembrarmos d'isto …
Depois quando envelhecermos
E nem os Deuses puderem
Dar côr ás nossas faces
E mocidade aos nossos collos,

Lembremo-nos, á lareira,
Cheiinhos de pesar

19

[6 October 1914]

The sea lies still. The winds moan secretly,
    Captives of Aeolus,
While Neptune barely ruffles the waters
    With the points of his trident,
And the beach is white and full of tiny
    Glinting lights beneath the bright sun.
I wish, Neaira, that the moment
    Here before us now had
The precise meaning of a sentence
    Visible in some book.
Then you would see how right I am
    When, without looking at you, I say
That things are the dialogue the gods
    Play at sharing with us.
If you could accept this simple fact,
    You would never again judge
Ordinary life to be either solemn or frivolous,
    Either light or serious,
Either false or true, but just this, divine
    And serene, and nothing more.

20

[c. 12 June 1914]

Neaira, let us walk together
Simply to remember later that we did ...
Later, when we grow old
And not even the Gods can
Put color in our cheeks
And restore youth to our hearts.

Seated by the fire, let us remember,
However sad we feel

O ser quebrado o fio,
Lembremo-nos, Neëra,
De um dia ter passado
Sem nos termos amado ...

21

Não pra mim mas pra ti teço as grinaldas
Que de hera e rosas eu na fronte ponho.
    Para mim tece as tuas
    Que as minhas eu não vejo.

Um para outro, mancebo, realisemos
A belleza improficua mas bastante
    De agradar um ao outro
    Plo prazer dado aos olhos.

O resto é o fado que nos vae contando
Pelo bater do sangue em nossas frontes
    A vida até que chegue
    A hora do barqueiro.

22

Vós que, crentes em Christos e Marias
Turvaes da minha fonte as claras aguas
    Só para me dizerdes
    Que ha aguas mais alegres

Banhando prados com melhores horas,—
D'essas outras regiões pra que fallar-me
    Se estas aguas e prados
    São de aqui e me agradam?

To find the thread broken,
Let us remember, Neaira,
That we did once spend a day
Without having loved each other ...

21   [30 July 1914]

Not for me but for you do I weave these garlands
Of ivy and roses that I place upon my head.
        You weave yours for me
        Since I cannot see my own.

Let us then, lad, give to each other
The futile but rather consoling beauty
        Of pleasing each other
        With the pleasure of looking.

The rest is the fate that counts off the days
In the pulsing of blood in our temples
        Until the hour comes,
        The hour of the boatman.

22   [9 August 1914]

You, believers in Christs and Marys
Who muddy the clear waters of my spring
        Purely to assure me
        That there are happier waters

Bathing meadows with better days—
Why speak to me of those other places
        If these waters and these meadows
        Are here now and are pleasure enough?

Esta realidade os deuses deram
E para bem real a deram externa.
　　Que serão os meus sonhos
　　Mais que a obra dos deuses?

Deixai-me a Realidade do momento
E os meus deuses tranquillos e immediatos
　　Que não moram no Incerto
　　Mas nos campos e rios.

Deixae-me a vida ir-se pagãmente
Acompanhada plas avenas tenues
　　Com que os juncos das margens
　　Se confessam de Pan.

Vivei vós vossos sonhos e deixae-me
O altar natural onde é meu culto
　　E a visivel presença
　　Dos meus proximos deuses.

Inuteis procos do melhor que a vida,
Deixae a vida aos crentes mais antigos
　　Que a Christo e a sua cruz
　　E Maria chorando.

Ceres, dona dos campos, me console
E Apollo e Venus, e Urano antigo
　　E os trovões, com o interesse
　　De irem da mão de Jove.

This is the reality the gods gave us
And, for good reason, they made them real.
	What are my dreams
	But the work of the gods?

Leave me the Reality of the moment,
Leave me my tranquil, immediate gods
	Who do not dwell in Uncertainty
	But in the fields and rivers.

Leave me to live my life paganly
Accompanied by the tenuous flutings
	With which the reeds on the banks
	Confess their allegiance to Pan.

You live your dreams and leave me
The natural altar at which I worship
	And the visible presence
	Of my nearby gods.

Failed procurers of something better than life,
Leave life to those believers more ancient
	Than Christ and his cross
	And Mary weeping.

Let Ceres, mistress of the fields, console me
And Apollo and Venus and ancient Uranus
	And the bolts of thunder, knowing
	That they come from the hand of Jove.

23

Não como ante donzella ou mulher viva
Com calôr na belleza humana d'ellas
 Devemos dar os olhos
 Á belleza immortal.

Eternamente longe ella se mostra
E calma e para os calmos adorarem
 Não de outro modo é ella
 Immortal como os deuses.

Que nunca a alegria transitoria
Nem a paixão que busca—porque cinge
 Devem olhar de nossos
 Olhos para a belleza.

Como quem vê um Deus e nunca ousa
Amal-o mais que como a um Deus se ama
 Deante da belleza
 Façamo-nos debeis.

Para outra cousa não a dão os deuses
Á nossa febre humana e vil da vida,
 Porisso a contemplemos
 N'um claro esquecimento.

E de tudo tiremos a belleza
Como a presença altiva e encoberta
 E o longinquo sorriso
 De quem assiste á vida.

23

We might gaze warmly on the human beauty
Of some living maiden or woman,
　　But never must we gaze thus
　　On immortal beauty.

Such beauty remains eternally remote
And calm, for only the calm to worship,
　　This is why such beauty is
　　Immortal like the gods.

Neither transient joy
Nor the passion it seeks—because it binds—
　　Should look with our eyes
　　Upon that beauty.

Like someone seeing a God but never daring
To love him more than one can love a God,
　　So it is with the beauty
　　That makes us bend the knee.

This is the reason why the gods bestow beauty
On our vile, human, feverish life,
　　The reason why, when we contemplate beauty,
　　We completely forget ourselves.

Let us find beauty in all things
With the haughty, hidden demeanor
　　And the distant smile
　　Of someone merely observing life.

24

Só esta liberdade nos concedem
    Os deuses: submettermo-nos
Ao seu dominio por vontade nossa.
    Mais vale assim fazermos
Porque só na ilusão da liberdade
    A liberdade existe.
Nem outro geito os deuses, sobre quem
    O eterno fado pesa,
Usam para seu calmo e possuido
    Convencimento antigo
De que é divina e livre a sua vida.
    Nós, imitando os deuses,
Tão pouco livres como elles no Olympo,
    Como quem pela areia
Ergue castelos para usar os olhos,
    Ergamos nossa vida
E os deuses saberão agradecer-nos
    O sermos tão como elles.

25

O rhytmo antigo que ha nos pés descalços
Esse rhythmo das nymphas copiado
    Quando sob arvoredos
    Batem o som da dança—

Pelas praias ás vezes, quando brincam
Ante onde a Apollo se Neptuno allia
    As crianças maiores,
    Tem semelhanças breves

Com versos já longínquos em que Horacio
Ou mais classicos gregos acceitavam

24
The gods grant us but one freedom:
          To submit ourselves
Of our own free will to their dominion.
          And it's best that we do,
Because freedom only exists
          In the illusion of freedom.
The gods, who bear the weight of Eternal fate,
          Have no other way
Of preserving their calm, confident,
          And very ancient belief
That their lives are divine and free.
          We, in imitation of the gods,
Enjoy as little freedom as they on Olympus.
          And like someone building castles
In the sand simply as a way of using his eyes,
          Let us build our lives,
And the gods will be grateful to us
          For being so very like them.

25   [9 August 1914]
The ancient rhythm to be found in bare feet,
A rhythm copied from the nymphs
          When, beneath the trees,
          They beat out the sound of their dances—

Or sometimes on the beaches, when the older children dance
At the very place where Neptune
          Joins with Apollo,
          They bear a slight resemblance

To those distant verses in which Horace
Or the more classical Greeks accepted

A vida por dos deuses
Sem mais preces que a vida.

Porisso á beira d'este mar, donzellas,
Conduzi vossa dança ao som de risos
Soberbamente antigas
Pelos pés nús e a dança

Emquanto sobre vós arqueia Apollo
Como um ramo alto o azul e a luz da hora
E ha o rito primitivo
Do mar lavando as costas.

26
Não porque os deuses findaram, alva Lydia, choro…
Mas porque nas boccas de hoje os nomes sobrevivem
Mortos sobrevivem, como nomes em pedras sepulchraes.
Por isso, Lydia, lamento
Que Venus em boccas christãs seja uma palavra dita,
Que Apollo seja um nome que usam quantos
Sequentes de Christo—e a crença lucida
Nos deuses puramente deuses,
Tenha passado e ficado, cinza do que era fogo,
Lama do que era agua reflectindo as arvores,
Tronco morto do que dava fructo e florescia.
Mas se chóro, não creio
Menos que ainda existo, como existem os deuses.

27
Passando a vida em vêr passar a de outros,
Botões de flôr de um esforço nunca aberto

Life as belonging to the gods
With life itself the only prayer.

And so, fair maidens, beside the sea,
Dance your dance to the sound of laughter,
    Proudly ancient
    In your bare feet and in your dance,

While, above you, Apollo draws a line of light
In the blue, like the arching branch of a lofty tree,
    While, below, the sea continues
    Its primitive ritual of washing the shore.

26   [1914]
I do not weep, fair Lydia, because the gods have died ...
But because in today's mouths their names, though dead, survive,
Survive like the names on gravestones.
    Which is why, Lydia, I regret
That Venus should be a word on Christian lips,
That Apollo should be a name used by many
Followers of Christ—and the lucid belief
    In gods who were purely gods
Should have vanished, leaving only ash that once was fire,
Mud that was once water mirroring trees,
The dead trunk of what once blossomed and bore fruit.
    But though I weep, I still believe
That I exist, just as the gods exist too.

27   [11 August 1914]
Spending one's life watching the lives of others pass,
Mere buds of an impulse that never opened

Na antiga semelhança com os deuses
   Que andam nos campos

A ensinar aos que as Parcas não ignoram
Como a vida se deve usar, e como
Ha outro uso que agricola dos campos
   E outro das fontes

Que beber d'ellas na hora da sêde.
Passando assim a vida, destruindo
O que fiamos hontem [...] *
   Penelopes tristes.

28
Deixemos, Lydia, a sciencia que não põe
Mais flores do que Flora pelos campos,
   Nem dá de Apollo ao carro
   Outro curso que Apollo.

Contemplação esteril e longinqua
Das cousas proximas, deixemos que ella
   Olhe até não ver nada
   Com seus cançados olhos.

Vê como Ceres é a mesma sempre
E como os louros campos entumesce
   E os cala prás avenas
   Dos agrados de Pan.

* Here, as elsewhere in this edition, missing text is indicated by an ellipsis inside brackets.

To reveal our former resemblance to the gods
    Strolling in the fields,

Teaching those whom the Fates are watching
How life should be spent, and how the fields
Have more than just agricultural uses,
    Just as the springs

Do not exist solely for us to quench our thirst.
A life spent thus, unpicking and destroying
What we wove yesterday […]
    Sad Penelopes.

28   [1914]
Let us ignore, Lydia, any science that fails to sow
More flowers in the meadows than Flora,
    Or to set Apollo's chariot
    On a different course.

Abandon science's remote, sterile contemplation
Of things near at hand and instead let it
    Gaze until it can see no more
    With its weary eyes.

Observe how Ceres is always the same
And how she ripens the blonde fields
    And bids them hush
    To hear Pan's sweet flute.

Vê como com seu geito sempre antigo
Aprendido no orige azul dos deuses,
As nymphas não socegam
Na sua dança eterna.

E como as hemadryades constantes
Murmuram pelos rumos das florestas
E atrazam o deus Pan
Na attenção á sua flauta.

Não de outro modo mais divino ou menos
Deve aprazer-nos conduzir a vida,
Quer sob o ouro de Apollo
Ou a prata de Diana.

Quer troe Jupiter nos ceus toldados,
Quer apedreje com as suas ondas
Neptuno as planas praias
E os erguidos rochedos.

Do mesmo modo a vida é sempre a mesma.
Nós não vemos as Parcas acabarem-nos.
Porisso as esqueçamos
Como se não houvessem.

Colhendo flores ou ouvindo as fontes
A vida passa como se temessemos.
Não nos vale pensarmos
No futuro sabido.

Que aos nossos olhos tirará Apollo
E nos porá longe de Ceres e onde
Nenhum Pan cace á flauta
Nenhuma branca nympha.

Observe how with their ancient gestures
Learned from the blue beginnings of the gods,
      The nymphs never rest
      From their eternal dancing.

And how the constant hamadryads keep up
Their murmurings along the forest paths
      And distract the god Pan
      From his flute-playing.

This is the way, be it more divine or less,
That we should choose to lead our life,
      Whether beneath the gold of Apollo
      Or the silver of Diana,

Whether Jupiter thunders forth from heavy skies,
Or Neptune pounds with his waves
      The flat beaches
      And the craggy rocks.

In the same way life carries on the same.
We do not notice the Fates destroying us,
      And so let us forget them
      As if they were not there.

Whether we're picking flowers or listening to springs,
Life passes as if we were afraid of it.
      But why bother thinking
      About the known future,

A future to which Apollo will blind us
And place us far from Ceres, a place
      Where no flute-playing Pan goes
      Hunting for pale-faced nymphs.

Só as horas serenas reservando
Por nossas, companheiros na malicia
De ir imitando os deuses
Até sentir-lhe a calma.

Venha depois com suas cans cahidas
A velhice, que os deuses concederam
Que esta hora por ser sua
Não soffra de Saturno

Mas seja o templo onde sejamos deuses
Inda que apenas, Lydia, pra nós proprios
Nem precisam de crentes
Os que de si o fôram.

29

N'este dia em que os campos são de Apollo
Verde colonia dominada a ouro,
Seja como uma dança dentro em nós
O sentirmos a vida.

Não turbulenta, mas com os seus rhythmos
Que a nossa sensação como uma nympha
Acompanhe em cadencias suas a
Disciplina da dança ...

Ao fim do dia quando os campos fôrem
Imperio conquistado pelas sombras
Como uma legião que segue marcha
Abdiquemos do dia,

Only by reserving the serene hours
For ourselves alone, companions in the game
     Of imitating the gods,
     Can we learn their calm.

Let old age come, then, with its sparse gray hairs
And may the gods grant that this hour,
     Being theirs, will not
     Allow Saturn to enter,

But will be the temple where we are the gods
Even if that temple, Lydia, is for us alone,
     Since those who are their own gods
     Have no need of believers.

29   [11 August 1914]

On this day when the fields belong to Apollo,
A green colony dominated by gold,
May our sense of being alive
     Be like a dance inside us.

Not turbulent, but with its own rhythms,
In which our senses, like a nymph's,
Keep time, beating their own cadences, with the
     Discipline of the dance …

At the end of the day, when the fields are
Like an empire conquered by the legions
Of shadows that come marching in,
     Let us abdicate from the day,

E na nossa memoria colloquemos,
Como um deus novo d'uma nova terra
Trazido, o que ficou em nós da calma
    Do dia passageiro.

30

É tão suave a fuga d'este dia,
Lydia, que não parece que vivemos.
    Sem duvida que os deuses
    Nos são gratos esta hora,

E em paga nobre d'esta fé que usamos
Na exilada verdade dos seus corpos
    Nos dão o alto premio
    De nos deixarem ser

Convivas lucidos da sua calma,
Herdeiros um momento do seu geito
    De viver toda a vida
    Dentro d'um só momento,

D'um só momento, Lydia, em que afastados
Das terrenas angustias recebemos
    Olympicas delicias
    Dentro das nossas almas.

E um só momento nos sentimos deuses
Immortaes pela calma que vestimos
    E a altiva indifferença
    Ás cousas transitorias.

And let us place in our memory—
like a new god brought from a new land—
what remains inside us of the calm
        Of that fleeting day.

30   [1914]
So gently, Lydia, does this day slip away,
We seem almost not to be living.
        The gods are clearly
        Well pleased with us.

And as noble reward for the faith we place
In the exiled truth of their bodies,
        They give us the fine prize
        Of allowing us to be

Lucid partakers of their calm,
Heirs for a moment of their way
        Of living a whole life
        Within a single moment,

A single moment, Lydia, in which, removed
From all earthly cares, our souls
        Are the happy recipients
        Of Olympian delights.

And for that one moment, we feel we are
Immortal gods, having put on their calm
        And their lofty indifference
        To all things transitory.

Como quem guarda a c'roa da victoria
Estes fanados louros de um só dia
    Guardemos para termos,
     No futuro enrugado,

Perenne á nossa vista a certa prova
De que um momento os deuses nos amaram
    E nos deram uma hora
    Não nossa, mas do Olympo.

31

Acima da verdade estão os deuses.
A nossa sciencia é uma falhada copia
    Da certeza com que elles
    Sabem que ha o Universo.

Tudo é tudo, e mais alto estão os deuses.
Não pertence á sciencia conhecel-os,
    Mas adorar devemos
    Seus vultos como ás flores,

Porque visiveis á nossa alta vista,
São tão reaes como reaes as flores
    E no seu calmo Olympo
    São outra Humanidade.

32

Não consentem os deuses mais que a vida.
Porisso, Lydia, duradouramente
    Façamos-lhe' a vontade
    Ao sol e entre flores.

Much as someone might keep a laurel wreath,
We will keep the faded laurels of this one day
        To have and to hold
        In the rumpled future,

As perennial proof, in our eyes,
That, for a moment, the gods loved us
        And gave us an hour belonging
        Not to us, but to Olympus.

31   [16 October 1914]

The gods are above the truth.
Our knowledge is but a flawed copy
        Of the certainty with which
        They know the Universe exists.

Everything is everything, and higher still are the gods.
Our knowledge is not equipped to know them,
        But we should worship
        Them as if they were flowers,

Since, visible to our lofty gaze,
They are as real as flowers are real,
        And on their calm Olympus
        They form another Humanity.

32   [17 July 1914]

The gods allow that only life exists,
So, Lydia, let us enduringly
        Obey their wishes
        In the sun, among flowers.

Camaleões pousados sobre as coisas
Tomemos sua calma e alegria
    Por côr da nossa vida
    Por uma arte do corpo.

Como vidros ás luzes transparentes
E deixando escorrer a chuva triste;
    Só mornos ao sol quente;
    E reflectindo um pouco.

33

As rosas amo dos jardins de Adonis,
Essas voluveis amo, Lydia, rosas,
    Que no dia em que nascem,
    No mesmo dia morrem.

A luz para ellas é eterna, porque
Nascem nascido já o sol, e acabam
    Antes que Apollo deixe
    O seu curso visivel.

Assim façamos nossa vida *um dia*.
Inscientes, Lydia, voluntariamente
    Que ha noite antes e após
    Do pouco que duramos.

34

Antes de nós nos mesmos arvoredos
Passava o vento, quando havia vento,
    E as folhas não mexiam
    De outro modo do que hoje.

Chameleonlike, perched on top of things,
Let us use their calm and joy
     To put color in our life
     And make of our body art.

Like windows transparent to the light
And letting the sad rain run down them;
     Warm only in the hot sun;
     And reflecting just a little.

33   [11 July 1914]
The roses I love in the gardens of Adonis,
Lydia, are the ephemeral kind, roses
     That die the day
     They are born.

Light for them is eternal, because
They are born when the sun is born,
     And die before Apollo
     Has completed his visible course.

Let us make of our life *one day*.
Choosing not to know, Lydia,
     That there is night before and after
     The brief span of our existence.

34   [8 October 1914]
Before we lived, the wind would blow,
When there was wind, through these same trees,
     And the leaves would stir
     No differently than now.

Passamos e agitamo-nos debalde.
Não fazemos mais ruído no que existe
    Do que as folhas das arvores
    Ou os passos do vento.

Tentemos pois com abandono assiduo
Entregar nosso esforço á Natureza
    E não querer mais vida
    Que a das arvores verdes.

Inutilmente parecemos grandes.
Salvo nós nada pelo mundo fóra
    Nos saúda a grandeza
    Nem sem querer nos serve.

Se aqui, á beira-mar, o meu indicio
Na areia o mar com ondas trez o apaga.
    Que fará na outra praia
    Em que o mar é Saturno?

35
Cada cousa a seu tempo tem seu tempo.
Não florescem no inverno os arvoredos,
    Nem pela primavera
    Têm branco frio os campos.

Á noite, que entra, não pertence, Lydia,
O mesmo ardor que o dia nos pedia.
    Com mais socego amemos
    A nossa incerta vida.

We pass and grow agitated, all in vain.
We make no more noise in the world
        Than the leaves of the trees
        Or the wind as it passes.

Let us try then with assiduous abandon
To surrender all our efforts to Nature
        And require no more life
        Than do the green trees.

We struggle pointlessly to appear great.
Apart from us, nothing in the wider world
        Bows to our greatness
        Or even serves us.

If here, on the seashore, with just three waves
The sea can wash away my footprint in the sand,
        What will it do on that other beach
        Where Saturn is the sea?

35   [30 July 1914]

Each thing in its time has its time.
The trees do not blossom in winter,
        Nor in the spring
        Are the fields cold white.

The coming night, Lydia, has none
Of the warmth the day asked of us.
        Let us love more calmly
        Our own uncertain life.

Á lareira, cançados não da obra
Mas porque a hora é a hora dos cansaços,
    Não forcemos a voz
    A estar mais que em segredo,

E casuaes, interrompidas sejam
Nossas palavras de reminiscencia
    (Não para mais nos serve
    A negra ida do sol).

Pouco a pouco o passado recordemos
E as historias contadas no passado
    Agora duas vezes
    Historias, que nos fallem

Das flores que na nossa infancia ida
Com outro fim no goso nós colhiamos
    E com outra sciencia
    No olhar lançado ao mundo.

E assim, Lydia, á lareira, como estando,
Deuses lares, alli na eternidade,
    Como quem compõe roupas
    O outr'ora compunhamos.

Nesse desassocego que o descanço
Nos traz ás vidas quando só pensamos
    N'aquillo que já fomos,
    E é noite sobre Ceres.

By the hearth, weary not from labor
But because it is the hour to feel weary,
        Let us not raise our voices
        Much above a whisper.

And let our words of reminiscence
Be casual, inconsequential
        (What else can they be after
        The sun's departure into darkness).

Let us, little by little, recall the past
And the stories told in the past,
        Now stories twice over,
        Stories that speak to us

Of the flowers that, in our vanished childhood,
We would pick with a different kind of pleasure
        And with a different knowledge
        In the way we looked at the world.

And so, Lydia, as we sit by the hearth,
Like household gods there for all eternity,
        Let us mend our pasts
        Like someone mending clothes.

In the disquiet that a moment's pause
Brings to our lives when we think only
        Of what we were,
        And night falls on Ceres.

36

Boccas roxas de vinho,
Testas brancas sob rosas,
Nús, brancos antebraços
Deixados sobre a mesa:

Tal seja, Lydia, o quadro
Em que fiquemos, mudos,
Eternamente inscriptos
Na consciencia dos deuses.

Antes isto que a vida
Como os homens a vivem,
Cheia da negra poeira
Que erguem das estradas.

Só os deuses soccorrem
Com seu exemplo aquelles
Que nada mais pretendem
Que ir no rio das cousas.

37

Tirem-me os deuses
Em seu arbitrio
Superior e urdido ás escondidas
Amôr, gloria e riqueza.

Tirem, mas deixem-me,
Deixem-me apenas
A consciencia lucida e solemne
Das cousas e dos seres.

36
Lips purple with wine,
Pale brows garlanded with roses,
Bare, white forearms
Resting on the table:

Let that, Lydia, be the picture
In which we remain, silent,
And eternally inscribed
On the consciousness of the gods.

Better that than life
As men live it,
Full of the black dust
They kick up along the roads.

The gods only help
By their example those
Who want nothing more than
To step into the river of things.

37
      May the gods,
      With their superior will
Woven in secrecy, take from me
      Love, glory, wealth.

      Let them take those
      And leave me only
The lucid, solemn consciousness
      Of things and beings.

Pouco me importa
Amor ou gloria.
A riqueza é um metal, a gloria é um echo
E o amôr uma sombra.

Mas a concisa
Attenção dada
Ás formas e ás maneiras dos objectos
Tem abrigo seguro.

Seus fundamentos
São todo o mundo,
Seu amôr é o placido universo.
Sua riqueza a vida.

A sua gloria
É a suprema
Certeza da solemne e clara posse
Das formas dos objectos.

O resto passa,
E teme a morte.
Só nada teme ou soffre a visão clara
E inutil do Universo.

Essa a si basta,
Nada desseja
Salvo o orgulho de ver sempre claro
Até deixar de vêr.

38

Feliz aquelle a quem a vida grata
Concedeu que dos deuses se lembrasse
E visse como elles

I care little for
Love or glory.
Wealth is a metal, glory an echo,
And love a mere shadow.

But the concise
Attention given
To the forms and manners of objects
Offers a safe haven.

Its foundations
Are the whole world,
Its love is the serene universe,
Its wealth life.

Its glory
Is the supreme
Certainty of a clear, solemn knowledge
Of the shapes of things.

Everything else passes
And fears death.
Only the clear, futile vision of the Universe
Neither fears nor suffers.

Sufficient unto itself,
It desires nothing,
Only the pride of always seeing clearly
Until it ceases to see.

38   [11/12 September 1916]
Happy the man to whom life kindly
Granted a knowledge of the gods
So that, like them, he could see

Estas terrenas cousas onde mora
Um reflexo mortal da immortal vida.
Feliz, que quando a hora tributaria
Transpor seu atrio porque a Parca corte
O fio fiado até ao fim,
Gosar poderá o alto premio
De errar no Averno grato abrigo
Da convivencia [...]
Mas aquelle que quer outro antepôr
Aos mais antigos Deuses que no Olympo
Seguiram a Saturno—
O seu blasphemo ser abandonado
Na fria expiação—até que os Deuses
De quem se esqueceu d'elles se recordem—
Erra, sombra inquieta, incertamente,
Nem o filho lhe põe na boca
O estygio obulo devido.
E sobre o seu corpo insepulto
Não deita terra o viandante.

39
Olho os campos, Neera,
Verdes campos, e penso
Em que virá um dia
Em que não mais os olhe.

Isto, se o meditar,
Me toldará os ceus
E fará menos verdes
Os verdes campos reaes.

Ah! Neera, o futuro
Ao futuro deixemos.

In the earthly things among which he lives
A mortal reflection of immortal life.
Happy the man who, when the tributary hour
Crosses his threshold, because Atropos has cut
        The thread spun out until its end,
        Can enjoy the high prize
        Of wandering through Avernus,
        That pleasant haven of companionship […]
But he who replaces with another
The older Gods who on Olympus
        Succeeded Saturn—
Whose blasphemous self was driven out
In chill atonement—until the Gods
Whom he forgot remember him—
He, an unquiet shade, is left to wander aimlessly
        With no child to place in his mouth
        The expected Stygian obol,
        And over whose unburied corpse
        No wayfarer will scatter earth.

39   [27 January 1917]
I look at the fields, Neaira,
These green fields, and think
That there will come a day
When I will no longer look at them.

This, were I to ponder it further,
Would cloud the skies
And make less green
These real green fields.

Ah! Neaira, let us leave
The future to the future.

                                                    65

O que não stá presente
Não existe pra nós.

Hoje não tenho nada
Senão os verdes campos
E o ceu azul por cima.
Seja isto todo a vida.

40
Deixa passar o vento
Sem lhe perguntar nada.
Seu sentido é apenas
Ser o vento que passa ...

Consegui que d'esta hora
O sacrifical fumo
Subisse até ao Olympo.
E escrevi estes versos
Pra que os deuses voltassem.

41
Só o ter flores pela vista fóra
Nas aleas largas dos jardins exactos
    Basta para podermos
    Achar a vida leve.

De todo o esforço seguremos quedas
As mãos. brincando, pra que nos não tome
    Do pulso, e nos arraste.
    E vivamos assim,

Only what is present
Exists for us.

All I have today
Are the green fields
And the blue sky above.
Let this be all of life.

40   [12 September 1916]
Let the wind pass by
Without asking it anything.
Its meaning is simply
Being the wind that passes …

This time I managed to send
The sacrificial smoke
Up to Olympus.
And I wrote these verses
To make the gods return.

41   [16 June 1914]
Simply seeing flowers everywhere,
Lining the broad paths of neat gardens
        Is enough for us
        To take life lightly.

Let us cling on with all our might, our hands
Firmly, playfully, by our sides, so that no one will grab
        Us by the wrist and drag us off.
        Yes, let us live like that,

Buscando o mínimo de dôr ou goso,
Bebendo a goles os instantes frescos,
　　Translucidos como agua
　　Em taças detalhadas,

Da vida pallida levando apenas
As rosas breves, os sorrisos vagos,
　　E as rapidas caricias
　　Dos instantes voluveis.

Pouco tão pouco pesará nos braços
Com que, exilados das supernas luzes,
　　Scolhermos do que fômos
　　O melhor pra lembrar

Quando, acabados pelas Parcas, fôrmos,
Vultos solemnes de repente antigos,
　　E cada vez mais sombras,
　　Ao encontro fatal

Do barco escuro no soturno rio,
E os nove abraços do horroso estygio,
　　E o regaço insaciavel
　　Da patria de Plutão.

Seeking the minimum of pain or pleasure,
Drinking each fresh moment sip by sip,
    Translucid as water
    In engraved goblets,

Taking from pallid life only
Brief roses, vague smiles,
    And the swift caresses
    Of the fleeting moments.

Little, so little will it weigh in the arms
With which, exiled from the divine light,
    We choose from what we were
    The better to remember

When, our lives cut short by Atropos, we set off,
Solemn and suddenly ancient figures,
    Ever more shadowlike,
    To our fateful encounter

With the dark boat on the gloomy river,
And the nine embraces of the Stygian cold,
    And the insatiable bosom
    Of Pluto's homeland.

Front cover of the inaugural issue of Athena

From Athena *(1924)*

Some of the odes featured in *Athena* are revised versions of earlier works.

42/I

Seguro assento na columna firme
    Dos versos em que fico,
Nem temo o influxo innumero futuro
    Dos tempos e do olvido;
Que a mente, quando, fixa, em si contempla
    Os reflexos do mundo,
D'elles se plasma torna, e á arte o mundo
    Cria, que não a mente.
Assim na placa o externo instante grava
    Seu ser, durando nella.

43/II

As rosas amo dos jardins de Adonis,
Essas volucres amo, Lydia, rosas,
    Que em o dia em que nascem,
    Em esse dia morrem.
A luz para ellas é eterna, porque
Nascem nascido já o sol, e acabam
    Antes que Apollo deixe
    O seu curso visivel.
Assim façamos nossa vida *um dia*.
Inscientes, Lydia, voluntariamente
    Que ha noite antes e após
    Do pouco que durámos.

44/III

O mar jaz; gemem em segredo os ventos
    Em Eolo captivos;
Só com as pontas do tridente as vastas
    Aguas franze Neptuno;
E a praia é alva e cheia de pequenos
    Brilhos sob o sol claro.

42/I   [1923–1924]

Seated securely on the solid pillar
        Of the verses in which I remain,
I have no fear of the endless future influx
        Of times and oblivion;
For the mind, when it steadfastly sees in itself
        The reflections of the world,
Becomes malleable clay, and it is the world
        That creates art, not the mind.
Just as the external instant engraves its being
        on the photographic plate, and there endures.

43/II   [11 July 1914]

The roses I love grow in the gardens of Adonis,
The ephemeral kind, Lydia, roses
        That die the day
        They were born.
Light for them is eternal, because
They are born when the sun is born,
        And die before Apollo
        Has completed his visible course.
Let us make of our life *one day*.
Choosing not to know, Lydia,
        That there is night before and after
        The brief span of our existence.

44/III   [1923–1924]

The sea lies still; the winds softly moan,
        Captives of Aeolus;
While Neptune barely ruffles the vast waters
        With the points of his trident;
And the beach is white beneath the sun and full
        Of tiny glittering lights.

Inutilmente parecemos grandes.
Nada no alheio mundo,
Nossa vista grandeza reconhece
Ou com razão nos serve.
Si aqui de um manso mar meu fundo indicio
Trez ondas o apagam,
Que me fará o mar que na atra praia
Echoa de Saturno?

45/IV

Não consentem os deuses mais que a vida.
Tudo pois refusemos, que nos alce
A irrespiraveis pincaros
Perennes sem ter flores.
Só de acceitar tenhamos a sciencia,
E, emquanto bate o sangue em nossas fontes,
Nem se engelha comnosco
O mesmo amor, duremos,
Como vidros ás luzes transparentes,
E deixando escorrer a chuva triste,
Só mornos ao sol quente,
E reflectindo um pouco.

46/V

Como si cada beijo
Fôra de despedida,
Minha Chloe, beijemo-nos, amando.
Talvez que já nos toque
No hombro a mão, que chama
Á barca que não vem senão vazia;
E que no mesmo feixe
Ata o que mutuos fomos
E a alheia somma universal da vida.

In vain we wish to appear great.
　　　For nothing in the indifferent world
Acknowledges our greatness
　　　Or deigns to serve us.
If just three of this sea's gentle waves
　　　Can wash away my deep footprint,
What will Saturn's booming sea do to me,
　　　When it breaks on that dark shore?

45/IV   [1923–1924]

The gods allow that only life exists.
Let us, then, reject whatever might raise us up
　　　To unbreathable, perennial
　　　but flowerless heights.
All our knowledge lies in accepting this,
So, while the blood still beats in our temples,
　　　And love does not wither
　　　Inside us, let us simply endure,
Like windows, transparent to the light,
And letting the sad rain run down them,
　　　Warm only in the hot sun,
　　　And reflecting just a little.

46/V   [17 November 1923]

　　　As if each kiss
　　　Were our last,
Let us embrace fondly, dear Chloe,
　　　For we may already feel
　　　On our shoulder the hand
Summoning the boat that always arrives empty,
　　　And that binds up in the same bundle
　　　All that we have been to one another
As well as the universal sum of other lives.

47/VI

O rythmo antigo que ha em pés descalços.
Esse rythmo das nymphas repetido,
    Quando sob o arvoredo
    Batem o som da dança,
Vós na alva praia relembrae, fazendo,
Que scura a spuma deixa; vós, infantes,
    Que inda não tendes cura
    De ter cura, responde
Ruidosa a roda, emquanto arqueia Apollo,
Como um ramo alto, a curva azul que doura,
    E a perenne maré
    Flue, enchente ou vasante.

48/VII

Ponho na activa mente o fixo exforço
    Da altura, e á sorte deixo,
    E a suas leis, o verso;
Que, quando é alto e regio o pensamento,
    Subdita a phrase o busca
    E o scravo rythmo o serve.

49/VIII

Quam breve tempo é a mais longa vida
E a juventude nella! Ah Chloe, Chloe,
    Si não amo, nem bebo,
    Nem sem querer não penso,
Pesa-me a lei inimploravel, doe-me
A hora invita, o tempo que não cessa,
    E aos ouvidos me sobe
    Dos juncos o ruido

47/VI

The ancient barefoot rhythm of the nymphs.
The rhythm they repeat and beat out
    When, beneath the trees,
    They gather to dance,
Like you, now, on the white beach darkened
By the breaking foam; you, children,
    Who still have no cure
    For there being a cure, respond
To the noisy circle, while, like a lofty branch,
Apollo draws an arc across the blue-gold vault,
    And high tide or low,
    The tide perennially flows.

48/VII

Into my active mind I pour all the effort
    Of the moment, leaving the verse
    To fate and its own laws;
For when the thought is lofty and regal,
    The subject words seek it out
    And the slave rhythm serves.

49/VIII

How brief is even the longest life,
Let alone its youth! Ah Chloe, Chloe,
    If I neither love nor drink,
    Nor, unthinkingly, think,
Still the unappealable law weighs on me, pains me,
As does the unvanquished hour and ceaseless time,
    And from the reeds
    A sound rises to my ears—

Na occulta margem onde os lirios frios
Da infera leiva crescem, e a corrente
    Não sabe onde é o dia,
    Sussurro gemebundo.

50/IX

Coroae-me de rosas.
Coroae-me em verdade
    De rosas—
Rosas que se apagam
Em fronte a apagar-se
    Tam cedo!
Coroae-me de rosas
E de folhas breves,
    E basta.

51/X

Melhor destino que o de conhecer-se
Não frue quem mente frue. Antes, sabendo,
    Ser nada, que ignorando:
    Nada dentro de nada.
Si não houver em mim poder que vença
As Parcas trez e as moles do futuro,
    Já me dêem os deuses
    O poder de sabe-lo;
E a belleza, increavel por meu sestro,
Eu gose externa e dada, repetida
    Em meus passivos olhos,
    Lagos que a morte sécca.

On the hidden bank where the cold lilies
Grow in the soft earth, and the stream
        That knows nothing of time—
        A mournful whisper.

50/IX

Crown me with roses
Yes, really, crown me
        With roses—
Roses that fade
On a brow fading
        All too fast!
Crown me with roses
And a few short-lived leaves,
        Nothing more.

51/X   [22 October 1923]

What better fate for one who has a mind
Than that of knowing himself. Better to know
        You are nothing, than to ignore it:
        Nothing within nothing.
While I have not the power to overcome
The three Furies and the formless future,
        The gods have given me
        The power to know this;
And the beauty my own fate would never create
I enjoy as a gift from beyond, reflected
        In my passive eyes, lakes
        That death will one day dry.

52/XI

Temo, Lydia, o destino. Nada é certo.
Em qualquer hora pode succeder-nos
    O que nos tudo mude.
Fora do conhecido é extranho o passo
Que proprio damos. Graves numes guardam
    As linhas do que é uso.
Não somos deuses: cegos, receemos,
E a parca dada vida anteponhamos
    Á novidade, abysmo.

53/XII

A flor que és, não a que dás, eu quero.
Porque me negas o que te não peço?
    Tempo ha para negares
    Depois de teres dado.
Flor, sê-me flor! si te colher avaro
A mão da infausta sphynge, tu perenne
    Sombra errarás absurda,
    Buscando o que não déste.

54/XIII*

Ólho os campos, Neera,
Grandes campos, e soffro
Já o frio da sombra
Em que não terei olhos.
A caveira antesinto
Que serei não sentindo,
Ou só quanto o que ignoro

---

* There are several versions of this ode, dated from 1915 to 1923. We have reproduced the version that appeared in *Athena* in 1924, incorporating the emendations found in the magazine's copy.

52/XI   [1923–1924]

I fear fate, Lydia. Nothing is certain.
At any moment something might happen
        That will change everything.
Beyond the known, every step we take
Is unknown. Grave-faced gods guard
        The boundaries of the usual.
We are not gods: we live blind and afraid,
And prefer the little life we are given
        To the new, the abyss.

53/XII   [c. 21 October 1923]

I want the flower you are, not the flower you give.
Why refuse me what I haven't even asked for?
        There'll be time enough to refuse
        Once you have given it.
A flower, be a flower for me! If plucked by the greedy hand
Of the ominous sphynx, you will be condemned
        To wander, an absurd, perennial shade,
        In search of what you did not give.

54/XIII   [25 December 1923]

I gaze with pleasure at the fields, Neaira,
The vast fields, and already I can feel
The chill of the shadows
Where I will have no eyes to see.
I can already sense the skull
I will become and yet not feel,
Or only if what I do not know

Me incognito ministre.
E menos ao instante
Chóro, que a mim futuro,
Subdito ausente e nullo
Do universal destino.

55/XIV

De novo traz as apparentes novas
Flores o verão novo, e novamente
    Verdesce a cor antiga
    Nas folhas redivivas.
Não mais, não mais d'elle o infecundo abysmo,
Que mudo sorve o que mal somos, torna
    Á clara luz superna
    A presença vivida.
Não mais; e a prole a que, pensando, dera
A vida da razão, em vão o chama,
    Que as nove chaves fecham
    Da Styge irreversivel.
O que foi como um deus entre os que cantam,
O que do Olympo as vozes, que chamavam,
    Scutando ouviu, e, ouvindo,
    Entendeu, hoje é nada.
Tecei embora as, que teceis, grinaldas,
Quem coroaes, não coroando a elle?
    Votivas as deponde,
    Funebres sem ter culto.
Fique, porém, livre da leiva e do Orco,
A fama; e tu, que Ulysses erigira,
    Tu, em teus septe montes,
    Orgulha-te materna,
Egual, desde elle, ás septe que contendem
Cidades por Homero, ou alcaica Lesbos,

Should unknowingly assist me.
And I weep, less for the moment
Than for my future self,
The absent, insignificant
Subject of the universal fate.

55/XIV   [22 October 1923]
Once more the new summer brings
The apparently new flowers, and
        Makes new and verdant
        The resurrected leaves.
No more, no more for him the barren abyss
That silently absorbs what we barely are, returning
        The lived life
        To the supernal light.
No more; and in vain they call to him, the offspring
To which, by thinking, he gave the life of reason,
        Locked away by the nine keys
        Of the irreversible Styx.
He who was like a god among those who sing,
He who heard the voices of Olympus calling,
        And listening heard and hearing,
        Understood, today is nothing.
Weave garlands then, those who can,
For who else would you crown if not him?
        Leave them as votive offerings,
        For one who had no religion.
However, free from the plowed field and the Underworld,
May his fame remain, and you, built
        By Ulysses on your seven hills,
        Can feel a maternal pride,
A city which, thanks to him, is equal to the seven that claim
To be Homer's birthplace, or Alceus's Lesbos,

Ou heptapyla Thebas
Ogygia mãe de Pindaro.

56/XV

Este, seu scasso campo ora lavrando,
Ora, solemne, olhando-o com a vista
De quem a um filho olha, gosa incerto
    A não-pensada vida.
Das fingidas fronteiras a mudança
O arado lhe não tolhe, nem o empece
Per que consilios se o destino rege
    Dos povos pacientes.
Pouco mais no presente do futuro
Que as hervas que arrancou, seguro vive
A antiga vida que não torna, e fica,
    Filhos, diversa e sua.

57/XVI

Tuas, não minhas, teço estas grinaldas,
Que em minha fronte renovadas ponho.
    Para mim tece as tuas,
    Que as minhas eu não vejo.
Se não pesar na vida melhor goso
Que o vermo-nos, vejamo-nos, e, vendo,
    Surdos conciliemos
    O insubsistente surdo.
Coroemo-nos pois una para os outros,
E brindemos unisonos á sorte
    Que houver, até que chegue
    A hora do barqueiro.

Or seven-gated Thebes,
Ogygian mother of Pindar.

56/XV   [16 November 1923]
This man, working his scant field,
Or else gazing at it solemnly like someone
Gazing at a son, he, all unknowing, enjoys
        The unconsidered life.
His plow remains unhampered by changes
To artificial frontiers, nor is he troubled
By whatever councils may rule over the fate
        Of patient peoples.
Existing little more in the present of the future
Than the weeds he pulled up, he lives securely
In the old life that will not return, but endures
        Like children, different and his own.

57/XVI   [c. 17 November 1923]
I weave these garlands for you, not me,
And place them newly woven upon my head.
        Weave yours for me,
        For mine I cannot see.
If no finer pleasure weighs on life than
That of looking at each other, then let us look,
        And silently accept
        Our silent insubsistence.
Let us then crown ourselves for others to see
And together toast in unison whatever fate
        Might bring, until the hour
        Of the boatman arrives.

58/XVII

Não queiras, Lydia, edificar no spaço
Que figuras vindouro, ou prometter-te
Amanhã. Cumpre-te hoje, não sperando.
 Tu mesma és tua vida.
Não te destines, que não és futura.
Quem sabe si, entre a taça que esvazias,
E ella de novo enchida, não te a sorte
 Interpõe o abysmo?

59/XVIII

Saudoso já d'este verão que vejo,
Lagrimas para as flores d'elle emprego
 Na lembrança invertida
 De quando hei de perdel-as.
Transpostos os portaes irreparaveis
De cada anno, me anticipo a sombra
 Em que errarei, sem flores,
 No abysmo rumoroso.
E colho a rosa porque a sorte manda.
Marcenda, guardo-a; murche-se commigo
 Antes que com a curva
 Diurna da ampla terra.

60/XIX

 Prazer, mas devagar,
Lydia, que a sorte áquelles não é grata
 Que lhe das mãos arrancam.
Furtivos retiremos do horto mundo
 Os depredandos pomos.
Não dispertemos, onde dorme, a erynnis
 Que cada goso trava.

58/XVII
[c. 1923]

Do not wish, Lydia, to build in that space
You imagine to be the future, or promise yourself
A tomorrow. Be fully yourself today, don't wait.
      You are your life,
Do not destine yourself, for you are not future.
Who can say if, between emptying your cup
And filling it again, fate will not have
      Interposed the abyss?

59/XVIII
[c. 1923]

Already nostalgic for the summer I see before me,
I shed tears for the flowers I pick
      In inverse memory
      Of when I must lose them.
Having crossed the irretrievable portals
Of each passing year, I anticipate the darkness
      In which I will wander, flowerless,
      In the murmurous abyss.
And, since fate ordains, I pick a rose
and watch it fading; come, fade with me
      Rather than with the diurnal
      Curve of the ample Earth.

60/XIX
[3 November 1923]

      Take your pleasures slowly,
Lydia, for it displeases fate to have pleasure
      Snatched from its hands.
Let us furtively steal our plundered apples
      From the orchard world.
Let us not awaken, where it sleeps, the Fury
      That impedes each pleasure.

Como um regato, mudos passageiros,
Gosemos escondidos.
A sorte inveja, Lydia. Emmudeçamos.

61/XX

Cuidas, invio, que cumpres, apertando
Teus infecundos, trabalhosos dias
 Em feixes de hirta lenha,
 Sem illusão a vida.
A tua lenha é só peso que levas
Para onde não tens fogo que te aqueça.
 Nem soffrem peso aos hombros
 As sombras que seremos.
Para folgar não folgas; e, se legas,
Antes legues o exemplo, que riquezas,
 De como a vida basta
 Breve, nem tambem dura.
Pouco usamos do pouco que mal temos.
A obra cança, o ouro não é nosso.
 De nós a mesma fama
 Ri-se, que a não veremos
Quando, acabados pelas parcas, formos,
Vultos solemnes, de repente antigos,
 E cada vez mais sombras,
 Ao encontro fatal—
O barco escuro no soturno rio,
E os nove abraços da frieza stygia
 E o regaço insaciavel
 Da patria de Plutão.

Let us, like silent voyagers on a stream,
        Take our pleasures secretly.
For fate is envious, Lydia. Best keep silent.

61/XX   [1923–1924]

Take care on the impassable roads you follow,
Clutching your fruitless, laborious days
        Like bundles of stiff firewood,
        With no illusions about life.
Your firewood is only a weight that you carry
To the place where no fire will warm you.
        The shadows we will become
        Carry no such weight.
In order to rest, do not rest; and, if you leave anything,
Leave neither money nor wealth, only the example
        Of how life, however brief,
        however transient, is enough.
We make so little use of the little we have.
Work is wearisome, the gold is not ours.
        Even fame itself
        Laughs at us, for we will not see it
When, snatched away by the Fates, we—
Vague, solemn shapes, grown suddenly ancient,
        And ever more shadowlike—
        Set out for the fatal encounter with
The dark boat on the grim river,
And the nine cold Stygian kisses
        And the insatiable embrace
        Of Pluto's homeland.

TRÊS ODES

Não só vinho, mas nêle o olvido, deito
Na taça: serei ledo, porque a dita
E' ignara. Quem, lembrando
Ou prevendo, sorrira?
Dos brutos, não a vida, senão a alma,
Consigamos, pensando; recolhidos
No impalpável destino
Que não spera nem lembra.
Com mão mortal elevo à mortal boca
Em frágil taça o passageiro vinho,
Baços os olhos feitos
Para deixar de ver.

Quanta tristeza e amargura afoga
Em confusão a streita vida! Quanto
Infortúnio mesquinho
Nos oprime supremo!
Feliz ou o bruto que nos verdes campos
Pasce, para si mesmo anónimo, e entra
Na morte como em casa;
Ou o sábio que, perdido
Na sciência, a fútil vida austera eleva
Além da nossa, como o fumo que ergue
Braços que se desfazem
A um céu inexistente.

A nada imploram tuas mãos já coisas,
Nem convencem teus lábios já parados,
No abafo subterrâneo
Da húmida imposta terra.
Só talvez o sorriso com que amavas
Te embalsema remota, e nas memórias
Te ergue qual eras, hoje
Cortiço apodrecido.
E o nome inútil que teu corpo morto
Usou, vivo, na terra, como uma alma,
Não lembra. A ode grava,
Anónimo, um sorriso.

Ricardo Reis.

CASAS EM MALAKOF madeira de DORDIO GOMES

3

Three Odes by Ricardo Reis, published in Presença

From Presença *(1927–1933)*

62

Não só vinho, mas nelle o olvido, deito
Na taça: serei ledo, porque a dita
    É ignara. Quem, lembrando
    Ou prevendo, sorrira?
Dos brutos, não a vida, senão a alma,
Consigamos, pensando; recolhidos
    No impalpavel destino
    Que não spera nem lembra.
Com mão mortal elevo á mortal bocca
Em fragil taça o passageiro vinho,
    Baços os olhos feitos
    Para deixar de ver.

63

Quanta tristeza e amargura afoga
Em confusão a streita vida! Quanto
    Infortunio mesquinho
    Nos opprime supremo!
Feliz o bruto que nos verdes campos
Pasce, para si mesmo anonymo, e entra
    Na morte como em casa;
    Ou o sabio que, perdido
Na sciencia, a futil vida austera eleva
Além da nossa, como o fumo que ergue
    Braços que se desfazem
    A um céu inexistente.

64

A nada imploram tuas mãos já coisas,
Nem convencem teus lábios já parados,
    No abafo subterraneo
    Da humida imposta terra.

62 [13 June 1926]

Into my cup I pour not just wine, but oblivion:
I will be merry because to be merry is to be ignorant.
    Who, when looking forward
    Or indeed back, would smile?
By thinking, we approach the souls.
Not the lives, of beasts; seeking refuge
    In the intangible destiny
    That neither hopes nor remembers.
With my mortal hand I raise to my mortal lips
A fragile cup of that fleeting wine,
    My eyes dull, eyes made
    To cease seeing.

63 [14 June 1926]

How easily overwhelmed are our narrow lives
By bitter grief and confusion! How many
    Petty misfortunes
    Bear down upon us!
Happy the beast grazing in the green fields,
Anonymous even to himself, and entering
    Death as if returning home;
    Or the wise man who, immersed
In knowledge, lifts his austere, futile life
Above our own, like so much smoke reaching up
    To a non-existent sky with
    Arms that instantly dissolve.

64 [May 1927]

Your hands, now mere things, no longer implore,
And your still lips can no longer persuade
    In the subterranean refuge
    Of the damp, heavy earth.

Só talvez o sorriso com que amavas
Te embalsama remota, e nas memorias
    Te ergue qual eras, hoje
    Cortiço apodrecido.
E o nome inutil que teu corpo morto
Usou, vivo, na terra, como uma alma,
    Não lembra. A ode grava,
    Anonymo, um sorriso.

65

O rastro breve que das hervas molles
Ergue o pé findo, o echo que ôco côa,
    A sombra que se adumbra,
    O branco que a nau larga—
Nem maior nem melhor deixa a alma ás almas,
O ido aos indos. A lembrança esquece.
    Mortos, inda morremos.
    Lydia, somos só nossos.

66

Já sobre a fronte vã se me acinzenta
O cabello do jovem que perdi.
    Meus olhos brilham menos.
Já não tem jús a beijos minha bocca.
Se me ainda amas, por amor não ames:
    Trahiras-me commigo.

67

Quando, Lydia, vier o nosso outomno
Com o inverno que ha nelle, reservemos
Um pensamento, não para a futura
    Primavera, que é de outrem.

Or perhaps all that remains, embalmed, remote,
Is your fond smile, and, in other people's memories,
　　　You rise up just as you once were,
　　　Not the rotting husk you now are.
And the futile name your dead body
Bore when alive on the earth, like a soul
　　　Remembers nothing. This ode
　　　The anonymous record of a smile.

65   [25 January 1928]
The brief trace left among the damp grass
By the vanished foot-fall, the echo that echoes in vain,
　　　The shadow that shadows itself,
　　　The white wake of the departed ship—
In no better or grander way, the soul leaves other souls,
Leaves the departed to the departing. Memory forgets.
　　　Even dead, we continue to die.
　　　Lydia, we exist only for ourselves.

66   [13 June 1926]
Already growing gray on my futile forehead
Is the hair of the young man I once was.
　　　My eyes shine less brightly.
My lips no longer deserve to be kissed.
If you still love me, then, please, out of love, don't:
　　　You would be betraying me with myself.

67   [13 June 1930]
When, Lydia, our autumn arrives along with
The winter it contains inside it, let us spare
A thought, not for the future
　　　Spring, which belongs to others,

Nem para o estio, de quem somos mortos,
Senão para o que fica do que passa—
O amarello actual que as folhas vivem
        E as torna differentes.

68

Tenue, como se de Eolo a esquecessem,
A brisa da manhã titila o campo,
        E ha começo do sol.
Não desejemos, Lydia, nesta hora
Mais sol do que ella, nem mais alta brisa
        Que a que é pequena e existe.

69

Para ser grande, sê inteiro: nada
        Teu exaggera ou exclue.
Sê todo em cada coisa. Põe quanto és
        No minimo que fazes.
Assim em cada lago a lua toda
        Brilha, porque alta vive.

Nor for the summer, for whom we are dead,
But for what remains of what is fleeting—
The present yellow in which the leaves are living
    And that makes them different.

68   [13 June 1930]
Gently, as if with no thought of Aeolus,
The morning breeze tickles the fields,
    And there is just a hint of sun.
At this moment, Lydia, let us not wish for
More sun than that, nor for a stronger breeze
    Than this small breeze here, now.

69   [14 February 1933]
To be great, be entire: no part of yourself
    Exaggerate or exclude.
Be whole in everything. Put all that you are
    Into the least that you do.
Thus in every lake the whole moon shines
    Because it lives on high.

Other Odes and Poems (1914–1935)

70

Quando Neptuno houver alongado
Até quasi aos bosques ao cimo da praia
Os seus braços com mãos ruidosas de espuma
    E eôlo houver
Largado por sobre o mar sob o azul
    Onde Apollo aquece
Os cavallos frescos dos ventos leves,
    Eu irei comtigo
Passear na altura cheirosa a mar
    Dos [...] altos
E concluir que esta vida é pouco
    Desde que os deuses
Fôram velados e os homens ingratos
Dos altares esquecidos tiraram todos
    Os ex-votos velhos,
Os ex-votos velhos que eram [...]
    [...]
    Que Christo e Maria
E de antes que a cruz pusesse a nudez
    Da sua seccura
De encontro ao ceu sempre velho e novo.

71

Pobres de nós que perdemos quanto
Sereno e forte nos dava a vida
O unico modo de a ter ...
    Pobres de nós
Creanças orphãs que mal se lembram
    De pae e mãe
E andam sósinhas na vida cega
    Sem ter carinhos
    Nem saber nada

70

When Neptune has reached out
His arms, his hands noisy with foam,
Almost as far as the woods above the beach,
        And Aeolus has
Unleashed upon the sea beneath the blue sky
        Warmed by Apollo
The fresh horses of his light winds,
        I will go with you,
And stroll at that salt-sea hour
        Of the high […]
And conclude that this life is but a poor thing
        Since the gods
Were covered over, and ungrateful men
Removed from the abandoned altars all
        The old ex-votos,
The old ex-votos that were […]
        […]
        Before Christ and Mary
And before the cross stood out stark
        And naked
Against the eternally old and new sky.

71

Alas, poor things, we have lost whatever serenity
And strength life gave us, which is,
After all, the only possible way to live life …
        Alas, poor things,
Orphaned children who can barely recall
        Father and mother,
And who walk alone through blind life,
        Knowing nothing of affection,
        And with no inkling of

De aonde vamos pla floresta,
Nem d'onde viemos pla Estrada fóra ...
E somos tristes, e somos velhos,
    E fracos sempre ...
      Sem que nos sirva.

72

Diana atravez dos ramos
Espreita a vinda de Endymion
Endymion que nunca vem,
Endymion, Endymion,
Lá longe na floresta ...

E a sua voz chamando
Suave atravez dos ramos,
Calma atravez dos ramos,
Endymion, Endymion ...

Assim choram os deuses ...

73

Sob estas arvores ou aquellas arvores
    Conduzi a dança,
Conduzi a dança, nymphas singelas
    Até ao amplo goso
Que tomaes da vida. Conduzi a dança
    E sê quasi humanas
Com o vosso goso derramado em rhythmos
    Em rhythmos solemnes
Que a nossa alegria torna maliciosos
    Para nossa triste
Vida que não sabe sob as mesmas arvores
    Conduzir a dança ...

Where we are heading through the forest,
Nor which path we followed to get here ...
And we are sad, and we are old,
        And always weak ...
        Which is no help at all.

72   [16 June 1914]

Through the branches Diana
Watches for the arrival of Endymion,
Endymion, who never comes,
Endymion, Endymion,
Far away in the forest ...

And her voice calling
Gently through the branches,
Calmly through the branches,
Endymion, Endymion ...

This is how the gods weep ...

73   [c. 11 July 1914]

Beneath these trees or those trees
        Come, lead the dance,
Lead the dance, O innocent nymphs,
        Into the ample pleasure
You take from life. Lead the dance
        And be almost human,
Your pleasure spilling over into rhythms,
        Solemn rhythms,
Rhythms our joy makes far too complicated
        For our sad life
Which, beneath these self-same trees,
        Does not know how to lead the dance ...

74

Ininterrupto e unido que o teu curso
Seja, e sereno para o mar distante.
          Teus versos não t'o parem.
          Interrompam-t'o apenas.
Mas conta tu as tuas proprias horas,
Á tua essencia dá-te incerta Iliada
          Que a gotas te não dá
          Tua legada vida ...

Condescendente p'ra contigo proprio,
Deixa aos outros artistas o fingir.
          Vive com a verdade
          Na imitação dos deuses
Que alheios a saber quanto quer delles
O céu do Fado, gosam a delicia
          Altiva de viverem
          Cada qual sua vida.

75

Aqui, sem outro Apollo do que Apollo,
Sem um suspiro abandonemos Christo
          E a febre de buscarmos
          Um deus dos dualismos.
E longe da christã sensualidade
Que a casta calma da belleza antiga
          Nos restitua o antigo
          Sentimento da vida.

74 [c. 11 July 1914]

May your journey to the distant sea
Be smooth, serene, unbroken.
        May your verses be no hindrance
        Or only a brief interruption.
But be sure to count your own hours,
Give your essence its own uncertain Iliad
        That the life bequeathed to you
        Gives you only drop by drop …

Be kind to yourself and leave it
To other artists to pretend and feign.
        Live with the truth,
        In imitation of the gods,
Who, oblivious to what might be required of them
By Fate's heaven, savor the proud delight
        Of each living
        His own life.

75 [11 August 1914]

Here, with no other Apollo but Apollo,
Without so much as a sigh, let us abandon Christ
        Along with our febrile search
        For a god of dualisms.
And far from the Christian sensuality
May the chaste calm of ancient beauty,
        Restore to us the ancient
        Sense of being alive.

76

Em Ceres anoitece.
Nos píncaros ainda
      Faz luz.
Sinto-me tão grande
N'esta hora solemne
      E vã
Que, assim como ha deuses
Dos campos, das flores
      Das seáras,
Agora eu quizera
Que um deus existisse
      De mim.

77

Emquanto ao longe os barbaros perturbam
Com a dos seus combates longa lista
      A parca e humilde chama
      De cada flebil vida,

E nem um palmo mais sequer conquistam
De riqueza ou de calma em suas almas,
      Nem são mais do que jogo
      Da ira […] dos deuses,

Quero, livre de humanas […]
De concordancia com o sentir de outros
      Mais firmemente minha
      Possuir minha vida.

76   [17 September 1914]

Darkness falls over Ceres.
On the mountaintops
        It is still light.
I feel so very grand
At this solemn
        And futile hour,
That, just as there are gods
Of the meadows, of the flowers,
        Of the wheatfields,
What I would like now
Is for there to be a god
        Of me.

77   [1914–1915]

While, far off, the barbarians,
With their long list of battles,
        Set the weak, humble flame
        Of every feeble life trembling,

And conquer not one iota more
Of wealth and calm in their own souls,
        And are no more than a plaything
        Of the wrath […] of the gods,

Free from human […]
And from the feelings of others,
        I want to own my own life
        To feel it more firmly mine.

78
Sob o jugo essencial e [...]
De Saturno, e de Jupiter seu filho,
Não vale que com Marte
Me aborreçam os momentos.

Calmo, solemnemente passageiro,
Dada ás cousas e á minha vida propria,
Procuro, não nos astros
Mas commigo viver-me.

E alheio a quanto sob os ceus distantes
Troa e anuvia a placidez das cousas,
Pertenço-me em segredo
Perante a Natureza.

79
Maior é quem a passo e passo avança
Na sua consciencia do universo
E palmo a palmo ganha
O dominio dos deuses.

Porque quanto mais certas vê as cousas
Mais por seu par os deuses o consentem
Até sentir seu corpo
Roçar corpos eternos.

Deixa, [...] meu, a ambição tua
De entre os homens por duque seres tido;
Deixa luzir p'ra outros
As lanças e as espadas.

78

Beneath the essential and [...] yoke
Of Saturn, and of Jupiter his son,
    In vain do they trouble my moments
    With the threat of Mars.

Calm, solemnly transient,
Given over to things and to my own life,
    I seek not to live among the stars
    But simply to live with myself.

And indifferent to whatever, beneath the distant skies,
May thunder and darken the placid nature of things,
    Secretly, before Nature,
    I belong solely to myself.

79
[1914–1915]

Greater is he who advances step by step
In his awareness of the universe
    And inch by inch reaches
    The domain of the gods.

For the more clearly he sees things
The more the gods see him as their equal
    Until, finally, he feels his body
    Brush their eternal bodies.

So, my [...], abandon all ambition
For other men to mistake you for a duke;
    Let others brandish
    Spears and swords.

De pelo gladio á gloria e á [...] ires ...
E a confiança em [...]
    A gloria onde te leva
    Mais que a onde não ha gloria?

80

Para os deuses as cousas são mais cousas.
Não mais longe elles veem, mas mais claro
    Na certa Natureza
    E a contornada vida ...

Não no vago que mal veem [...]
Orla mysteriosamente os seres,
    Mas nos detalhes claros
    [...] estão seus olhos.

A Natureza é só uma superficie.
Na sua superficie ella é profunda
    E tudo contém muito
    Se os olhos bem olharem.

Aprende pois, tu, das christãs angustias,
Ó traidor á multiplice presença
    Dos deuses, a não teres
    Veus nos olhos nem na alma.

81

Não batas palmas deante da belleza
Não se sente a belleza demasiado.
    Saibamos como os deuses
    Sentir divinamente.

For if you use the sword as your path to glory …
And place your trust in […]
> Where will that glory take you?
> Only to where there is no glory.

80 [1914–1915]

For the gods, things are simply things.
They see no further, but see more clearly
> In precise Nature
> And circumscribed life …

They see not the barely discernible vagueness […]
That mysteriously encircles all beings,
> But fix their eyes […]
> Only on the clear details.

Nature is nothing but surface.
But within that surface it is deep
> And there is much to see
> If one's eyes know how to look.

So, you with your Christian anxieties,
O traitor of the multiple presence
> Of the gods, learn not to wear
> A veil over either eyes or soul.

81 [12 February 1915]

Do not applaud in the presence of beauty,
Do not feel beauty too intensely.
> Let us learn, like the gods,
> To feel divinely.

Ao vêr o bello, lembra-te que morre.
E que a tristeza d'esse pensamento
    Torne elevada e calma
    A tua admiração.

E se é estatua ou de Pindaro alta estrophe
Em quem teus olhos são abandonados
    Não te esqueças de que essa
    Belleza não é viva.

Sempre ao bello uma cousa ha-de faltar
Para que seja triste contemplal-o
    E que nunca se possa
    Bater palmas ao vel-o ...

Calma é a belleza. Ama-a calmamente.
Os dons dos deuses como um deus acceita
    E terás tua parte
    Do nectar dado aos calmos.

82

Felizes, cujos corpos sob as arvores
    Jazem na humida terra,
Que nunca mais soffrem o sol, ou sabem
    Das mudanças da lua.
Verta Eolo a caverna inteira sobre
    O orbe esfarrapado.
Apedreje Neptuno as planas praias
    E os erguido rochedos,
Tudo lhe é nada, e o proprio pecureiro
    Que passa, finda a tarde,
Sob a arvore onde jaz quem foi a sombra
    Imperfeita de um deus,

When you see beauty, remember it will die,
And may the sadness of that thought
        Elevate and calm
        Your admiration.

And if it's a statue or a fine verse by Pindar
To which you have abandoned your gaze,
        Do not forget that such
        Beauty is not alive.

There is always something lacking in beauty
And so there is a sadness about it,
        Which means you should never
        Applaud when you do see it ...

Beauty is very calm. So love it calmly.
If you can accept the gifts of the gods like a god,
        You will have your share
        Of the nectar given only to the calm.

82   [1 June 1916]

Happy are those whose bodies lie beneath
        The trees in the damp earth,
Those who will never again feel the sun's heat, or follow
        The changes of the moon.
Aeolus can unleash all the winds from his cave
        Onto the whole ragged globe,
Neptune can batter the smooth beaches
        And the sheer cliffs,
And it will be as nothing, and even the shepherd—
        Strolling past at close of day
Beneath the tree where lies one who was the imperfect
        Shadow of a god—

Não sabe que os seus passos vão cobrindo
        O que podia ser,
Se a vida fosse sempre a vida, a gloria
        De uma belleza eterna.

83
Os jogadores de xadrez

Ouvi contar que outrora, quando a Persia
        Tinha não sei qual guerra,
Quando a invasão ardia na Cidade
        E as mulheres gritavam,
Dois jogadores de xadrez jogavam
        O seu jogo continuo.

Á sombra de ampla arvore fitavam
        O taboleiro antigo,
E, ao lado de cada um, esperando os seus
        Momentos mais folgados,
Quando havia movido a pedra, e agora
        Esperava o adversario,
Um pucaro com vinho refrescava
        A sua sobria sêde.

Ardiam casas, saqueadas eram
        As arcas e as parêdes,
Violadas, as mulheres eram postas
        Contra os muros cahidos,
Trespassadas de lanças, as creanças
        Eram sangue nas ruas ...
Mas onde estavam, perto da cidade,
        E longe do seu ruido,
Os jogadores de xadrez jogavam
        O jogo do xadrez.

Has no idea that his feet are treading upon
    What could have been,
If life were always life, the glory
    Of an eternal beauty.

83   [1 June 1916]
The Chess Players

I've heard it said that once, when Persia
    Was engaged in some war or other,
When the invaders had set the City ablaze,
    And women were screaming,
Two chess players calmly continued
    Their never-ending game.

They sat in the ample shade of a tree, eyes trained
    On their ancient board,
And beside each player, for those moments
    Of ease between moves,
While each waited for their opponent
    To make the next move,
There stood a jug of wine to cool
    their sober thirst.

Houses were burning, treasures had been
    Looted and walls demolished,
Women who had been raped were left
    Slumped against the fallen walls,
While their children, skewered by spears, were just
    So much blood on the streets ...
But the chess players, near the city,
    Yet far from the noise of war,
Continued unperturbed, still playing
    Their game of chess.

Inda que nas mensagens do ermo vento
    Lhes viessem os gritos,
E, ao reflectir, soubessem com acerto
    Que por certo as mulheres
E as tenras filhas violadas eram
    Nessa distancia proxima,
Inda que, no momento que o pensavam,
    Uma sombra ligeira
Lhes passasse na fronte alheada e vaga,
    Breve seus olhos calmos
Volviam sua attenta confiança
    Ao taboleiro velho.

Quando o rei de marfim está em perigo,
    Que importa a carne e o osso
Das irmãs e das mães e das creanças?
    Quando a torre não cobre
A retirada da rainha branca,
    O saque pouco importa.
E quando a mão confiada leva o cheque
    Ao rei do adversario,
Pouco pesa na alma que lá longe
    Estejam morrendo filhos.

Mesmo que, de repente, sobre o muro
    Surja a sanhuda face
D'um guerreiro invasor, e breve deva
    Em sangue alli cahir
O jogador solemne de xadrez,
    O momento antes d'esse
É ainda entregue ao jogo predilecto
    Dos grandes indiff'rentes.

Caiam cidades, soffram povos, cesse
    A liberdade e a vida,

Even though the screams were borne to them
       In messages carried on the empty winds,
And even though, on reflection, they knew
       For certain that their wives
And tender daughters were being raped
       Just that short distance away,
Even though, when they thought this,
       A very light shadow
Passed over their vague, distracted brows,
       It was not long before
Their calm eyes returned their attention
       To that old board.

When the ivory king is in danger,
       What do the flesh and blood
Of sisters and mothers and children matter?
       When the rook cannot cover
The white queen's retreat, who cares
       If the city is being sacked?
And when a hand confidently places
       The opponent's king in check,
It hardly weighs on the soul that, far off,
       Children are dying.

Even if, suddenly, over the wall, there appeared
       The furious, frowning face,
Of a war-like invader, even if soon afterwards,
       The solemn chess player
Were to fall, all drenched in blood,
       The previous moment
Would still be devoted to the favored game
       Of the utterly indifferent.

Cities may fall, people may suffer, life
       And liberty may cease,

Os haveres tranquillos e avitos
       Ardam e que se arranquem,
Mas quando a guerra os jogos interrompa,
       Esteja o rei em cheque,
E o de marfim peão mais avançado
       Prompto a comprar a torre.

Meus irmãos em amarmos Epicuro
       E o entendermos mais
De accordo com nós-proprios que com elle,
       Aprendamos na historia
Dos calmos jogadores de xadrez
       Como passar a vida.

Tudo o que é serio pouco nos importe,
       O grave pouco pese,
O natural impulsa dos instinctos
       Que ceda ao inutil goso
(Sob a sombra tranquila do arvoredo)
       De jogar um bom jogo.

O que levamos d'esta vida inutil
       Tanto vale se é
A gloria, a fama, o amor, a sciencia, a vida,
       Como se fosse apenas
A memoria de um jogo bem jogado
       E uma partida ganha
       A um jogador melhor.

A gloria pesa como um fardo rico,
       A fama como a febre,
O amor cança, porque é a serio e busca,
       A sciencia nunca encontra,
E a vida passa e dóe porque o conhece …
       O jogo do xadrez

Possessions, peacefully acquired or inherited,
    May be burned or stolen,
But when war interrupts a game, be sure
    That the king is in check,
And the most advanced of those ivory pawns
    Is ready to redeem the rook.

My brothers in loving Epicurus
    And in understanding him more
In accordance with ourselves than with him,
    Let us learn from the story
Of those coolheaded players of chess
    How to live our lives.

Let us care little about all serious things,
    Let grave matters weigh lightly,
And let the natural impulse of the instincts
    Be to surrender to the futile pleasure
(Beneath the tranquil shade of the trees)
    Of playing a game well.

It doesn't matter what we take from this futile life
    Whether it be
Glory, fame, love, knowledge, life,
    Or the mere
Memory of a game well played
    And of how once
    We beat a better player.

Glory weighs like a heavy burden,
    Fame like a fever,
Love wearies because it is serious and never satisfied,
    While knowledge is never found,
And life passes and grieves to know that it is passing ...
    The game of chess, though,

Prende a alma toda, mas, perdido, pouco
    Pesa, pois não é nada.

Ah, sob as sombras que sem qu'rer nos amam,
    Com um pucaro de vinho
Ao lado, e attentos só á inutil faina
    Do jogo do xadrez,
Mesmo que o jogo seja apenas sonho
    E não haja parceiro,
Imitemos os persas desta historia,
    E, emquanto lá por fora,
Ou perto ou longe, a guerra e a patria e a vida
    Chamam por nós, deixemos
Que em vão nos chamem, cada um de nós
    Sob as sombras amigas
Sonhando, elle os parceiros, e o xadrez
    A sua indifferença.

84

Prefiro rosas, meu amor, á patria,
    E antes magnolias amo
    Que fama e que virtude.

Logo que a vida não me cance, deixo
    Que a vida por mim passe
    Logo que eu fique o mesmo.

Que importa áquelle a quem ja nada importa
    Que um perca e outro vença,
    Se a aurora raia sempre,

Se cada anno com a primavera
    Apparecem as folhas
    E com o outomno cessam?

Occupies the whole soul and, if lost, weighs
    Little, because it is nothing.

Ah, sitting in the shade which, all unknowing, loves us,
    With a jug of wine beside us,
And deeply engaged only in the pointless task
    Of playing a game of chess,
Even if the game is merely a dream
    And there is no other player,
Let us imitate the Persians in that story,
    And whenever, elsewhere,
Near or far, war and homeland and life
    Call to us, let them
Call to us in vain, while each of us
    Sits in the friendly shade, dreaming,
The player of his opponents, and the chess
    Of its indifference.

84 [1 June 1916]

I prefer roses, my love, to my country,
    And I love magnolias
    More than fame and virtue.

As long as life does not weary me,
    I will let life pass me by,
    As long as I remain the same.

What does it matter to one who no longer cares
    If someone loses and another wins,
    As long as the sun always rises,

If, every year, when the spring returns,
    The leaves appear
    And in autumn fall?

O resto, as outras cousas que os humanos
    Accrescentam á vida,
    Que me augmentam na alma?

Nada, salvo o desejo de indiff'rença
    E a confiança molle
    Na hora fugitiva.

85

Segue o teu destino,
Rega as tuas plantas,
Ama as tuas rosas.
O resto é a sombra
De arvores alheias.

A realidade
Sempre é mais ou menos
Do que nós queremos.
Só nós somos sempre
Eguaes a nós-proprios.

Suave é viver só.
Grande e nobre é sempre
Viver simplesmente.
Deixa a dôr nas aras
Como ex-voto aos deuses.

Vê de longe a vida.
Nunca a interrogues.
Ella nada pode
Dizer-te. A resposta
Está além dos Deuses.

As for the rest, in what way do they augment the soul,
    Those other things
    We humans add to life?

In nothing, apart from a desire for indifference
    And an easy confidence
    In the fleeting hour.

85   [1 July 1916]

Follow your destiny,
Water your plants,
Love your roses.
The rest is the shade
From other people's trees.

Reality
Is always more or less
Other than what we want.
Only we are always
The same as ourselves.

How sweet it is just to live,
How great and noble always
Simply to live.
Leave sorrow on the altars,
A votive offering to the gods.

View life from afar.
And never question it,
For it has nothing
To tell you. The answer
Lies beyond the gods.

Mas serenamente
Imita o Olympo
No teu coração.
Os deuses são deuses
Porque não se pensam.

86

Não a ti, mas aos teus, odeio, Christo.
Tu não és mais que um deus a mais no eterno
        Pantheon que preside
        Á nossa vida incerta.

Nem maior nem menor que os novos deuses,
Tua sombria fórma dolorida
        Trouxe algo que faltava
        Ao numero dos divos.

Porisso reina a par de outros no Olympo,
Ou pela triste terra se quizeres
        Vae enxugar o pranto
        Dos humanos que soffrem.

Não venham, porém, stultos teus cultores
Em teu nome vedar o eterno culto
        Das presenças maiores
        E parceiras da tua.

A esses, sim, do amago eu odeio
Do crente peito, e a esses eu não sigo,
        Supersticiosos leigos
        Na sciencia dos deuses.

Instead, serenely
Imitate Olympus
In your heart.
The gods are gods because
They do not think about themselves.

86   [9 October 1916]

It isn't you I hate, Christ, but your followers.
You are merely another god in the eternal
        Pantheon that presides
        Over our uncertain life.

Neither greater nor smaller than the new gods,
Your somber, sorrowful figure
        Brought with it something
        The other gods lacked.

That is why you reign with others on Olympus,
Or on the sad earth should you choose
        To come and dry the tears
        Of us suffering humans.

Do not, however, let your dull worshippers
Use your name to banish the eternal cult
        Of those greater presences
        Of whom you are one.

It is those dull followers I hate from the depths
Of my believing heart, and them I do not follow,
        Superstitious laymen
        In their knowledge of the gods.

Ah, augmentae, não combatendo nunca.
Inriquecei o Olympo, aos deuses dando
    Cada vez maior força
    Plo número maior.

Basta os males que o Fado as Parcas fez
Por seu intuito natural fazerem.
    Nós homens nos façamos
    Unidos pelos deuses.

87

Soffro, Lydia, do medo do destino.
Qualquer pequena cousa de onde pode
Brotar uma ordem nova em minha vida,
    Lydia, me aterra.

Qualquer cousa, qual seja, que transforme
Meu plano curso da existência, embora
Para melhores cousas o transforme,
    Por transformar

Odeio, e não o quero. Os deuses dessem
Que ininterrupta minha vida fôsse
Uma planicie sem relevos, indo
    Até ao fim.

A gloria embora eu nunca haurisse, ou nunca
Amor ou justa stima dessem-me outros,
Basta que a vida seja só a vida
    E que eu a viva.

Ah, increase and enrich Olympus,
With no need for conflict, giving the gods
    Ever greater power
    Through greater numbers.

We have enough evils with those intuitive
Evils committed by Fate and the Furies.
    Let us humans band together
    Bound by the gods.

87   [26 May 1917]

I suffer, Lydia, from a fear of fate.
The tiniest thing from which might
Spring some new order in my life
    Terrifies me, Lydia.

Anything, whatever it is, that changes
The smooth course of my existence, even
If those changes are for the better,
    Because I simply hate

Change, and do not want it. May the gods
Make mine a life without interruptions,
A flat, uneventful plain, stretching out
    Until the end.

Even if I never taste glory or indeed love
Nor enjoy the due esteem of other people,
It is enough that life be simply life
    And that I live it.

88

Eu nunca fui dos que a um sexo o outro
No amor ou na amizade preferiram.
Por igual a belleza eu apeteço
    Seja onde for, belleza.

Pousa a ave, olhando apenas a quem pousa
Pondo querer pousar antes do ramo;
Corre o rio onde encontra o seu retiro
    E não onde é preciso.

Assim das differenças me separo
E onde amo, porque o amo ou não amo,
Nem a innocencia innata de quem ama
    Me é postergada nisto.

Não no objecto, no modo está o amor,
Logo que a ame, a qualquer cousa amo.
Meu amor nella não reside, mas
    Em meu amor.

Os deuses que nos deram este rumo
Tambem deram a flôr pra que a colhessemos
E com melhor amor talvez colhamos
    O que pra usar buscamos.

89

Não sem lei, mas segundo leis diversas
Entre os homens reparte o Fado e os deuses
    Sem justiça ou injustiça
Prazeres, dores, gozos e perigos.

88 [After 19 May 1917]

I was never one of those who, in love
Or friendship, preferred one sex or another.
I embrace beauty wherever I find it
    Simply as beauty.

The bird alights, barely looking at where it is alighting,
The desire to alight being more important than the branch;
The river flows wherever it finds its natural home
    Not where it needs to go.

This is how I distance myself from differences
And when I love, regardless of whether I do or don't love,
This still allows room for the innate innocence
    Of one who loves.

In love it is not the object that matters, but the manner,
And as long as I love, I can love anything,
My love lies not in the thing I love, but
    In my love.

The same gods who gave us this advice
Also gave us the flowers to pick
And let us perhaps with greater love choose
    What we seek to use.

89 [17 November 1918]

Fate and the gods do not share out among men
Pleasures, sorrows, delights, and dangers
    Fairly or unfairly,
Not at random, but according to diverse rules.

Bem ou mal, não terás o que mereces.
Querem os deuses do destino abrigo.
　　　　Nós confiantes dos deuses
E nem os deuses sabem do Destino.

Porque até aos deuses toda a acção é clara
E é boa ou má, feita para a julgarmos,
　　　　Porque o fado não tem
Leis nossas com que reja a sua lei.

Quem é rei hoje, amanhã scravo cruza
Com o scravo de ontem que é depois rei.
　　　　Sem razão um cahiu,
Sem causa nelle o outro ascenderá.

Não em nós, mas dos deuses no capricho
E nas sombras p'ra além do seu dominio
　　　　Está o que somos, e temos,
A vida e a morte do que somos nós.

Se te apraz mereceres, que te apraza
Por mereceres, não porque te o Fado
　　　　Dê o premio ou a paga
De com constancia haveres merecido.

Dubia é a vida, inconstante o que a governa.
O que esperamos nem sempre acontece
　　　　Nem nos falha sempre,
Nem ha com que a alma uma ou outra cousa spere.

Torna teu coração digno dos deuses
E deixa a vida incerta ser quem seja.
　　　　O que te acontecer
Acceita. Os deuses nunca se rebellam.

For good or ill, you will not receive what you deserve.
The gods try to seek shelter in destiny.
      Neither we who trust in the gods,
Nor even the gods themselves, know what Destiny is.

Because even to the gods every action is clear,
Either good or bad, and left to us to judge.
      Because fate does not have
Our rules with which to govern theirs.

Whoever is king today will be a slave tomorrow,
And walk past yesterday's slave and king-to-be.
      One fell without cause,
And the other will rise up for no reason.

What we are lies not in us, but at the whim of the gods
And in the darkness that lies beyond their domain,
      Leaving us only with what we have,
Namely, the life and death of what we are.

If it pleases you to win prizes, then, fine, enjoy
Your prizes, not because Fate gave you
      The prize or the reward
That you might actually have deserved to win.

Life is uncertain, and what rules it is inconstant.
What we hope for does not always happen
      Nor does it always fail us,
Nor can the soul expect one thing or the other.

Make your heart worthy of the gods
And let uncertain life be what it will.
      Whatever happens to you,
Accept it. For even the gods do not rebel.

Nas mãos inevitaveis do destino
A roda rapida soterra hoje
    Quem hontem viu o ceu
Do transitorio auge do seu gyro.

90

Antes de ti era a Mãe Terra scrava
Das trevas supernas que da alma nascem
    E cahem sobre o mundo
    Porque atraz o sol brilha.

A realidade ao mundo devolveste
Que haviam os christãos fechado na alma
    E as portas reabriste
    Por onde aurora o carro

Ou Phebo guie e os dois irmãos celestes
Quando no extremo mastro á noite luzem,
    Mais valham que um luzeiro
    Na ponta de um pau secco.

Restituiste a Terra á Terra. E agora
És parte corporal da propria terra,
    Ou sombra [...]
    Erras nas sombras frias,

Mas ao ouvir-te os povos com que auroras
Do abysmo os incolas as tristes frontes
    Erguem e sentem deuses
    Caminhar pelas sombra.

In the inevitable hands of destiny
The fast-turning wheel will bury today
        Whoever, yesterday, glimpsed the sky
Of the fleeting zenith of its gyre.

90   [17 November 1918]
Before you existed, Mother Earth was a slave
To the supernal darknesses born of the soul
        That fall upon the world because
        Behind them comes the bright sun.

You restored to the world the reality
To which Christians had closed their souls
        And reopened the gates
        Through which Aurora or Phoebus drives

Their chariot and then those two celestial siblings,
When they blaze at night above the tallest mast,
        Shine brighter than a lantern
        Held aloft on the end of a stick.

You restored the Earth to the Earth. And now
You are a physical part of the earth itself
        Or, a shadow […]
        You wander among cold shadows,

But on hearing you, the inhabitants of the abyss
On whom you shed light raise their sad faces,
        Sensing they can hear gods
        Strolling in the darkness.

E eis que de nova luz o abysmo se enche
E um ceu raia a cobrir o absorto fundo
        Da fauce mysteriosa
        Que traga o fim da vida.

91
Uma após uma as ondas apressadas
Enrolam o seu verde movimento
        E chiam a alva spuma
        No moreno das praias.

Uma após uma as nuvens vagarosas
Rasgam o seu redondo movimento
        E o sol aquece o spaço
        Do ar entre as nuvens scassas.

Indifferente a mim e eu a ella,
A natureza d'este dia calmo
        Furta pouco ao meu senso
        De se esvahir o tempo.

Só uma vaga pena inconsequente
Para um momento á porta da minha alma
        E após fitar-me um pouco
        Passa, a sorrir de nada.

92
Manhã que raias sem olhar a mim,
Sol que luzes sem qu'rer saber de eu ver-te,
        É para mim que sois
        Reais e verdadeiros.

And thus it is that new light fills the abyss
And a sky dawns, covering up the rapt depths
    Of the mysterious maw
    That swallows up the end of life.

91   [23 November 1918]
One after another, the hurrying waves
Repeat their green unfurlings
    And send the white foam
    Hissing over the brown sand.

One after another the slow clouds
Drift roundly across the sky
    And the sun warms the airy
    Space between them.

As indifferent to me as I to her,
Nature, on this calm day,
    Does little to distract my sense
    Of time slipping away.

Only a vague inconsequential sorrow
Pauses briefly at the door to my soul,
    Then, after looking at me for a moment,
    Moves on, smiling at nothing.

92   [23 November 1918]
Day that dawns without a glance in my direction,
Sun that shines whether I can see you or not.
    For me, though, you, day and sun,
    Are both so real and so true.

Porque é na opposição ao que eu desejo
Que sinto real a natureza e a vida.
    No que me nega sinto
    Que existe e eu sou pequeno.

E nesta consciencia torno ao grande
Como a onda, que as tormentas atiraram
    Ao alto ar, regressa
    Pesada a um mar mais fundo.

93

Cedo de mais vem sempre, Chloe, o hynverno.
É sempre prematuro, inda que o spere
    Nosso hábito, o esfriar
    Do desejo que houve.

Não entardece que não morra o dia.
Não nasce amor ou fé em nós que não
    Morra com isso ao menos
    O não amar ou crer.

Todo o gesto que o nosso corpo faz
Com o repouso anterior contrasta.
    Nesta má circunstancia
    Do tempo eternos somos.

Só sabe da arte com que viva a vida
Aquelle que, de tão contínua usal-a,
    Furte ao tempo a victoria
    Das mudanças depressa,

Because it is in opposition to what I wish
That I feel life and nature to be real.
        Only in those things that quite ignore me
        Do I feel I exist and how very small I am.

And knowing this, I turn to what is large and great,
Just as a wave, which the storms hurl up
        Into the high air, falls back
        Heavily into a far deeper sea.

93   [7 July 1919]

The winter, Chloe, always comes too soon,
Is always premature, even if, out of habit,
        We expect it, that cooling
        Of what was once desire.

For evening to come the day must die.
No love or belief can be born in us
        Without the death at least
        Of unlove or unbelief.

Every gesture our bodies make
Contrasts with our former state of repose.
        In this unfortunate aspect
        Of time we are eternal.

Only one who, by continually practicing
the art with which he lives his life, only he
        Is quick enough to snatch
        Victory from such changes,

E entardecendo como um dia trópico,
Até ao fim inevitavel guie
Uma egual vida, súbito
Precípite no abysmo.

94

No momento em que vamos pelos prados
E o nosso amor é um terceiro alli,
Que usurpa que saibamos
Um ao certo do outro,

Nesse momento, em que o que vemos mesmo
Sem o vermos na propria essencia entra
Da nossa alma commum—
Lydia, nesse momento

De tão sentir o amor não sei dizer-t'o,
Antes, se fallo, só dos prados fallo
E põe-se musica ao meu
Eros connosco invisivel.

95

Na fuga inutil dos penosos dias
Que pensando vivemos,
Perdemos, com a vida sem proveito,
O proprio pensamento,
Porque, quando não praz a vida, como
Pode aprazer pensal-a?
Sabio o que busca como não perder-se
Da vida meditando,
Mas com a vida o pensamento juncta
Meditando antes como

And like the evening of a day in the tropics,
He steers an untroubled life
    To its inevitable, sudden,
    Precipitous plunge into the abyss.

94   [7 July 1919]
In the moment when we head off to the fields
And our love is there like a third presence,
    Usurping our ability
    Properly to know each other,

In that moment, when what we see—even
Without seeing it—enters the very essence
    Of our shared soul—
    Lydia, in that moment

I feel love too deeply to put it into words,
Instead, if I speak, I speak only of the fields
    And thus there's a kind of music to my
    Eros—to us invisible.

95   [10 July 1919]
In the futile passing of the painful days
    We live by thinking,
We lose, in that profitless life,
    Our own thoughts,
Because if life does not please us, what pleasure
    Can be gained from thinking about it?
Wise is the man who finds a way not to waste his life
    By meditating on life.
Instead, combining life and thinking,
    He meditates on how

Viver que como comprehender a vida.
  Stulta a obra que busca
Saber da vida mais que como usal-a
  Ou como, bem perdendo
A alta luz, o verdor do campo, e o canto
  Das aves, ir na sombra
Com passos cheios de reminiscencia
  Para o seu fim exiguo.

96
Mas dia a dia
Com lapso gradual vae hora a hora
A vida vã tornando-se mais fria,
Vae descorando a face,
E a alma, acompanhando.

Ah, saibamos mostrar
Á vida a força de a acceitar,
Indifferentes tanto
Ao riso como ao pranto,
E, spectadores de nós proprios, nada
Na nossa consciencia elucidada.

97
Cumpre a lei, seja vil ou vil tu sejas.
Pouco pode o homem contra a externa vida.
    Deixa haver a injustiça.
    Nada mudes que mudas.

Não tens mais reino que a doada mente.
Essa, em que és servo, grato o Fado e os Deuses,
    Governa, até á fronteira,
    Onde a vontade finge.

To live life rather than on how to understand it.
    Foolish the work that seeks
To understand life rather than use it
    Or that, ignoring
The lofty light, the green fields, and the birdsong,
    Walks in the shade,
With steps filled with reminiscences,
    Towards its paltry end.

96   [26 May 1920]

But day by day,
Slipping gradually away, hour by hour,
Vain life is growing ever colder,
The color fading from its cheeks,
With the soul keeping it company.

Ah, let us learn how to show life
We have the strength to accept it,
Facing the laughter and the tears
With equal indifference, and, spectators of ourselves,
Conscious in our enlightened minds that we are nothing.

97   [29 January 1921]

Obey the law, however base you or it may be.
A man can do little to defend himself from external life.
    Let injustice be.
    Nothing you change will change.

Your only kingdom is the mind you were given.
The mind, to whom you are enslaved, thanks to Fate and the Gods,
    That governs as far as the frontier
    Where the will ceases its pretend existence.

Ahi vencido, tu por vencedores
Os grandes deuses e o Destino ostentas.
  Não ha a dupla derrota
  De derrota e vileza.

Assim penso, e esta subita justiça
Com que queremos moderar as cousas,
  Expillo, como a um servo
  Intromissôr da mente.

Se nem de mim posso ser dono, como
Quero ser dono ou lei do que acontece
  Onde me a mente e corpo
  Não são mais do que parte?

Basta-me que me baste, e o resto gyre
Na orbita prevista, em que até os deuses
  Gyram, soes centros servos
  De um movimento externo.

98
Um verso repete
Uma briza fresca,
O verão nas hervas,
E vazio soffre ao sol
O atrio abandonado.

Ou, no hynverno, ao longe
Os cimos de neve,
Á lareira toadas
Dos contos herdados,
E um verso a dizel-o.

142

There, vanquished, with, as you yourself attest,
The great gods and Destiny as your vanquishers,
    You at least avoid the double defeat
    Of defeat and baseness.

Or so I think, and the sudden justice
With which we try to control things
    I summarily dismiss, as if it were a servant
    Caught pilfering from the mind.

If I cannot even be master of myself, how
Can I hope to be master or law of what happens
    Where my mind and my body
    Play only a small part?

Let me be satisfied with what I have, and leave the rest
To follow the predictable orbit, followed even by the gods,
    The suns, centers and servants
    Of an external movement.

98   [29 January 1921]

A line of verse repeats
A cool breeze,
The summer among the grasses,
The empty abandoned courtyard
Baking in the sun.

Or, in the winter, the distant
Snow-capped peaks.
By the fireside, old songs and
Stories passed down to us
And a poem telling the tale.

Os deuses concedem
Poucos mais prazeres
Que estes, que são nada.
Mas tambem concedem
Não querermos outros.

99

Tornar-te-has só quem tu sempre foste.
O que te os deuses dão, dão no começo.
     De uma só vez o Fado
     Te dá o fado, que és um.

A pouco chega pois o exforço posto
Na medida da tua força nata—
     A pouco, se não foste
     Para mais concebido.

Contenta-te com seres quem não podes
Deixar de ser. Inda te fica o vasto
     Ceu p'ra cobrir-te, e a terra,
     Verde ou secca a seu tempo.

100

Em vão procuro o bem que me negaram.
As flores dos jardins herdadas de outros
Como hão de mais que perfumar de longe
     Meu desejo de tel-as?

The gods grant us few
Such pleasures, even though
These pleasures are nothing.
But they also grant that
We will want no others.

99 [12 May 1921]

You will only become the person you always were.
What the gods give you, they give at the start.
        Only once does Fate give you
        Your fate, and that is what you are.

Any efforts you make come to so little, depending
As they do on the strength you were born with—
        Yes, they come to very little, unless
        You were intended for greater things.

Content yourself with being the person
You can never cease to be. You still have
        The vast sky to cover you, and the earth,
        Green or parched according to the season.

100 [12 May 1921]

In vain I seek the good that was denied me.
How can the flowers of gardens bequeathed
By others do more than perfume from afar
        My desire to have them?

101

Não quero a fama, que commigo a teem
  Erostrato e o pretor
Ser olhado de todos—que se eu fosse
  Só bello, me olhariam.
O fausto repudio, porque o compram.
  O amor, porque acontece.
Amigo fui, talvez não contente,
  Porém nato e sem erro.

102

Pequeno é o espaço que de nós separa
O que havemos de ser quando morrermos.
Não conhecemos quem será o morto
  De hoje que então nos morra.

Só o passado, comum a nós e a elle,
Será indicio de que a nossa alma
Persiste e como antiga ama, conta
  Historia esquecidas ...

Se pudessemos pôr o pensamento
Com exacta visão dentro de vida
Que havemos de ter naquella hora,
  Extranhos olhariamos

O que somos, cuidando vêr um outro
E o spaço temporal que hoje habitamos
Luz onde nossa alma nasceu
  Alheia antes de a termos.

101
[12 May 1921]

I do not want fame, I leave that to others,
  To Herostratus and the praetor,
To be gawped at by everyone—which would happen
  Even if I were merely handsome.
I reject all pomp, because it can be bought.
  Love, because it merely happens.
I have been a friend, and although not perhaps content,
  Predestined to live without a stain.

102
[31 January 1922]

It is very small the space separating us
From what we will be when we die.
We do not know who among us
  Will be today's dead.

Only the past, common to us both,
Will provide proof that our soul
Persists and continues, like an old nanny,
  To tell forgotten stories ...

If we could, in our thoughts, paint
An exact picture of the life that would,
At that moment, be ours, we would
  Gaze, bewildered,

At who we are, as if we were someone else
And the temporal space we inhabit today
Were the light where our soul was born,
  Unknown to us until it was ours.

103

Cada um cumpre o destino que lhe cumpre,
E deseja o destino que deseja;
  Nem cumpre o que deseja,
  Nem deseja o que cumpre.

Como as pedras na orla dos canteiros
O Fado nos dispõe, e alli ficamos;
  Que a Sorte nos fez postos
  Onde houvemos de sel-o.

Não tenhamos melhor conhecimento
Do que nos coube que de que nos coube.
  Cumpramos o que somos.
  Nada mais nos é dado.

104

Quero versos que sejam como joias
Para que durem no porvir extenso
  E os não macule a morte
  Que em cada cousa a espreita,

Versos onde se esquece o duro e triste
Lapso curto dos dias e se volve
  Á antiga liberdade
  Que talvez nunca houvemos.

Aqui, nestas amigas sombras postas
Longe, onde menos nos conhece a historia
  Lembro os que urdem, cuidados,
  Seus descuidados versos.

103

We each fulfill the destiny we are given to fulfill
And we each desire the destiny we desire;
    We neither fulfill our desire
    Nor desire what we fulfill.

Fate arranges us like the stones bordering
A flower bed, and there we stay;
    It was Chance that placed us
    Where we were meant to be.

We have no better understanding
Of what is our due beyond its being our due.
    Let us be what we are.
    Nothing more is given to us.

104

I want verses that are like jewels
So that they last into the vast future
    Unsullied by the death that
    Lurks inside all things.

Verses where one forgets the harsh, sad,
Brief passing of the days and returns
    To the former freedom
    We possibly never had.

Here, among these friendly far-flung shadows
Where least is known about our history,
    I recall those who carefully
    Weave their careless verses.

E mais que a todos te lembrando, screvo
Sob o vedado sol, e, te lembrando,
    Bebo, immortal Horacio,
    Superfluo, á tua gloria …

105

    Sob a leve tutella
    De deuses descuidosos,
Quero gastar as concedidas horas
    D'esta fadada vida.

    Nada podendo contra
    O ser que me fizeram,
Desejo ao menos que me haja o Fado
    Dado a paz por destino.

    Da verdade não quero
    Mais que a vida; que os deuses
Dão vida e não verdade, nem talvez
    Saibam qual a verdade.

106

    Meu gesto que destrue
    A mole das formigas,
Tomal-o-hão ellas por de um ser divino;
Mas eu não sou divino para mim.

    Assim talvez os deuses
    Para si o não sejam,
E só de serem do que nós maiores
Tirem o serem deuses para nós.

And remembering you above all others,
I sit writing in the banished sun, and, remembering,
    I raise my cup, superfluously,
    To you, immortal Horace, to your glory ...

105   [c. 5 August 1923]
    Beneath the light protection
    Of the neglectful gods,
I wish to spend the hours of the predestined life
    They have granted me.

    Since I can do nothing
    About the being they made of me,
I wish at least that Fate will have given
    As my destiny, peace.

    All I want of truth
    Is life; for the gods
Give life, not truth, and may not even
    Know what truth is.

106   [c. 5 August 1923]
    The hand with which
    I destroy this anthill,
The ants will assume belongs to some divine being;
But I do not consider myself in the least divine.

    Perhaps the gods do not consider
    Themselves to be divine either.
And only because they are older than us
Do they believe they are our gods.

Seja qual fôr o certo,
Mesmo para com esses
    Que cremos serem deuses, não sejamos
    Inteiros numa fé talvez sem deuses.

107

Quero, da vida, só não conhecel-a.
Bastam, a quem o Fado poz na vida,
    As formas successorias
    Da vida insubsistente.

Pouco serve pensar que são eternos
Os nossos nadas com que na alma amamos
    Os outros pobres nadas
    Que [...]
Gratos aos deuses, menos pla incerta
Posse do Sonhado certo, recolhamos
    A mercê passageira
    De instantes que não duram.

108

Nada me dizem vossos deuses mortos
Que eu haja de apprender. O Crucifixo
    Sem amor e sem odio
    Do meu [...] afasto.

Que tenho eu com as crenças que o Christo
Curvado o torso a mim, latino, evoca?
    Mais com o sol me entendo
    Que com essas verdades ...

Whatever the truth of the matter,
Let us not give ourselves over
Wholeheartedly to a possibly baseless, godless faith
Even in those gods we believe to be gods.

107   [6 August 1923]

All I want of life is not to know it.
Anyone whom Fate has set down in life must accept
        The various successive forms
        Taken by substanceless life.

There is little point in believing to be eternal
The nothings with which, in our soul, we love
        Other poor nothings
        That […]
Grateful to the gods, rather than for the uncertain
Possession of a certain Fantasy, let us take comfort
        In the fleeting mercy
        Of instants that do not last.

108   [c. 6 August 1923]

Your dead gods have nothing to tell me
That I do not already know. The Crucifix,
        I drive from my […]
        Feeling neither love nor hate.

What do I care about the beliefs evoked
By that Christ who bends over me, a Latin?
        I have more in common with the sun
        Than I do with those truths …

Que o sejam ... Que a mim mais não foi dado
Que uma visão das cousas que ha na terra
    E uma razão incerta,
    E um saber que não dura ...

109

Não quero as offerendas
Em que, mau grado vosso,
Negaes-me o que me daes.
Daes-me o que perderei,
Chorando-o, duas vezes,
Por vosso e meu, perdido.

Antes vós, sem m'o dardes
M'o promettaes, que a perda
Será mais na sperança
Que na recordação.

Não terei mais desgosto
Que o contínuo da vida,
Vendo que com os dias
Tarda o que spera, e é nada.

110

Vossa formosa juventude leda,
Vossa felicidade pensativa,
Vosso modo de olhar a quem vos olha,
    Vosso não conhecer-vos—

Tudo quanto vós sois, que vos semelha
Á vida universal que vos esquece,
Dá carinho de amor a quem vos ama
    Por serdes não lembrando

If truths they be ... For all I was ever given
Was a vision of the things that exist on earth
    And a somewhat wavering mind,
    And a knowledge that does not endure ...

109   [2 September 1923]

I do not want the gifts
Which, given unwillingly,
You refuse even as you give them.
You give me what I will lose,
Weeping twice over
For your loss and for mine.

Better not to give it to me at all
But merely to promise; then the loss
Would be more of the hope
Than of the memory.

I will suffer no worse sorrow
Than the continuation of life,
For as the days pass, the hoped-for thing
Never comes, and, besides, is nothing.

110   [2 September 1923]

Your lovely, laughing youth,
Your pensive happiness,
Your way of looking at whoever looks at you,
    Your lack of self-knowledge—

Everything you are, that makes you so like
The universal life that gives no thought to you,
Fills with loving affection those who love you
    For not even considering

Quanta egual mocidade a eterna praia
De Chronos, pae injusto da justiça,
Ondas, quebrou, deixando á só memoria
    Um branco som de spuma.

111

Não canto a noite porque no meu canto
O sol que canto acabará em noite.
    Não ignoro o que esqueço.
    Canto por esquecel-o.

Pudesse eu suspender, inda que em sonho,
O Apollineo curso, e conhecer-me,
    Inda que louco, gemeo
    De uma hora imperecivel!

112

Não quero recordar nem conhecer-me.
Somos de mais se olhamos em quem somos.
    Ignorar que vivemos
    Cumpre bastante a vida.

Tanto quanto vivemos, vive a hora
Em que vivemos, egualmente morta
    Quando passa connosco,
    Que passamos com ella.

Se sabel-o não serve de sabel-o
(Pois sem poder que vale conhecermos?),
    Melhor vida é a vida
    Que dura sem medir-se.

How, on the eternal beach of Chronos,
That unjust father of justice, waves have broken
Over many equally lovely youths, leaving to memory only
    A white sound of foam.

111   [2 September 1923]

I do not sing of night because in my song
The sun of which I sing will end in night.
    I know what I have forgotten.
    And I sing in order to forget it.

If only, even in my dreams, I could stop
Apollo's course and know myself,
    However mad, to be the twin
    Of one imperishable hour!

112   [2 September 1923]

I do not want to remember or to know myself.
We just get in the way if we look into who we are.
    Not knowing we are alive
    Is quite enough of life.

The hour in which we live is just as alive
As we are, and also equally dead
    When it passes along with us
    As we pass along with it.

If knowing this is of no help in knowing this
(Because otherwise, what's the point of knowing ourselves?)
    The best life is the life
    Lived out unmeasured.

113

A abelha que, voando, freme sobre
A colorida flôr, e pousa, quasi
　　Sem differença d'ella
　　Á vista que não olha,

Não mudou desde Cecrops. Só quem vive
Uma vida com ser que se conhece
　　Envelhece, distincto
　　Da especie de que vive.

Ella é a mesma que outra que não ella.
Só nós—ó tempo, ó alma, ó vida, ó morte!—
　　Mortalmente compramos
　　Ter mais vida que a vida.

114

Dia após dia a mesma vida é a mesma.
　　O que decorre, Lydia,
No que nós somos como em que não somos
　　Egualmente decorre.
Colhido, o fructo deperece; e cahe
　　Nunca sendo colhido.
Egual é o fado, quer o procuremos,
　　Quer o speremos. Sorte
Hoje, Destino sempre, e nesta ou nessa
　　Forma alheio e invencivel.

113   [2 September 1923]

The bee that trembles, hovering, above
The bright flower, and rests there,
     Bee and flower barely distinguishable
     To the unperceptive eye,

Has not changed since Cecrops. Only someone who lives
A life as would a human being who knows himself, only he
     Grows old, and is thus distinct
     From others of his own species.

The bee is the same as any other bee.
Only we—O time, O soul, O life, O death!—
     Purchase with our mortality
     The right to have more life than life.

114   [2 September 1923]

Day after day, the same life is the same life.
     What happens, Lydia,
To what we are as well as to what we are not
     Happens anyway.
Once picked, the fruit rots, and falls
     If never picked.
Fate is the same, whether we seek it out
     Or simply wait. What is Chance today
Is also still our Destiny, and regardless of what form
     It takes, is both irrelevant and irresistible.

115

Flores que colho, ou deixo,
Vosso destino é o mesmo.

Via que sigo, chegas
Não só a onde eu chego.

Nada somos que valha
Somol-o mais que em vão.

116

Pequena vida consciente, sempre
Da repetida imagem perseguida
Do fim inevitável, a cada hora
    Sentindo-se mudada,

E, como Orpheu volvendo á vinda esposa
O olhar algoz, para o passado erguendo
A memoria pra em maguas o apagar
    No barathro da mente.

117

    De uma só vez recolhe
    Quantas flores puderes.
Não dura mais que até á morte o dia.
    Colhe de que recordes.

    A vida é pouco e cerca-a
    A sombra e o sem-remedio.
Não temos regras que comprehendamos,
    Subditos sem governo.

115   [c. 2 September 1923]

Whether I pick you or leave you, flowers,
Your destiny remains the same.

You, path that I follow, are heading
For other destinations, not just mine.

We are nothing that is of any worth
And are therefore doubly worthless.

116   [22 October 1923]

Our little conscious life, eternally
Pursued by the repeated image
Of the inevitable end, and with each hour
        Feeling itself changed,

And, like Orpheus turning his fatal backward gaze
On his wife, always dredging up memories
Of the past so as to drown it in sorrows
        In the chasm of the mind.

117   [24 October 1923]

        Once and for all gather as
        Many flowers as you can.
The day lasts only until its death.
        Gather in order to remember.

        Life is brief and besieged
        By darkness and the inevitable.
Having no rules we can understand, we are
        Subjects without a ruler.

Gosa este dia como
Se a Vida fôsse nelle.
Homens nem deuses fada, nem destina
Senão o que ignoramos.

118

A folha insciente, antes que a propria morra
    Para nós morre, Chloe,
Para nós, que sabemos que ella morre
    Assim, Chloe, assim
Antes que os proprios corpos, que empregamos
    No amor, ella envelhece.
Assim, diversos, somos, inda jovens,
    Só a mutua lembrança.
Ah, se o que somos é sempre isto, e apenas
    Uma hora é o que somos,
Com tal furia nessa hora nos usemos
    Que arda sua lembrança
Como vida, e nos beijemos, Chloe,
    Como se, findo o beijo
Unico, houvesse de ruir a subita
    Mole do morto mundo.

119

Se em verdade não sabes (nem sustentas
Que sabes) que ha na vida mais que a vida,
Porque com tanto exforço e cura tanta,
    Operoso a não vives?

Porque, sem paraíso que appeteças,
Amontoas riquezas, nem as gastas,
É para teu cadaver que amontoas?
    Gosas menos que ganhas.

Enjoy this day as if your
Very life depended on it.
Neither men nor gods decide our fate, and predestine
Us only for what we do not know.

118   [c. 27 October 1923]
Before it dies, the leaf, all unknowing,
    Has already died for us, Chloe,
For us, who know full well that it will die,
    Thus, Chloe, thus,
Before these our bodies, which we use in love,
    The leaf is growing old.
Thus, though different, though still young,
    We act as a mutual reminder.
Ah, if that is all we always are, and have only
    An hour to be just that,
Then with what fury must we use that hour
    So that the memory of it
Will burn like life itself, then, let us kiss, Chloe,
    As if, once that one kiss
Were done, the whole vast edifice of the dead world
    Would crumble into dust.

119   [29 October 1923]
If you truly do not know (or even pretend
To know) that there is more to life than life,
Why, given all your efforts and labors,
    Do you work so hard at not living?

Why, with no particular paradise in your sights,
Do you heap up money, but never spend it?
Are you hoarding it solely for your corpse to enjoy?
    Your pennies outweigh pleasure.

Ah, se não tens que esperes, salvo a morte,
Não cures mais que do preciso exforço
Para passar incolume na vida
    De [...]
Sim, gosas. Mas mais rico és que ditoso
Se só para o que perdes gosas,
Menos te o exforço onerara,
    Sem elle [...]
Ah servidão irreprimivel, nada
Da indole humana subsiste, que sabes
Que morre toda, e gasta-se nas obra
    [...]
Mas respondes-me: e os poemas que screves
A quem os dá futuro? a obra obriga
E o homem só por semear semeia
    O que o Destino manda

Egoista de um futuro que não é seu.

120
Tam cedo passa tudo quanto passa!
Morre tam jovem ante os deuses quanto
    Morre! Tudo é tam pouco!
Nada se sabe, tudo se imagina.
Circumda-te de rosas, ama, bebe
    E cala. O mais é nada.

121
Não inquiro do anonymo futuro
    Que serei, poisque tenho,
Qualquer que seja, que vivel-o. Tiro
    Os olhos do vindouro.

Ah, if you don't have what you expect, apart from death,
All you achieve with your efforts and labors
Is to pass through life unscathed
        By [...]
Yes, you enjoy life. But you're richer than you are happy
If you take pleasure only in what you lack,
You would be less bowed down by the effort,
        Without it [...]
Ah, irrepressible servitude, nothing
That is human survives, you must know
That everything dies, and one grows old in the doing
        [...]
In response, you say: what about the poems you write,
What future do they have? Work calls,
And a man sows purely for the sake of sowing
        Whatever Destiny decides

The egotist of a future not his own.

120   [3 November 1923]
How soon everything that passes passes!
All who die in the sight of the gods die so young!
        Everything is so very brief!
We know nothing, we imagine everything.
Surround yourself with roses, love, drink
        And say nothing. For there is nothing more.

121   [4 November 1923]
I do not enquire of the anonymous future
        What I will be, given that,
Whatever it is, I will have to live it. I look away
        From what is to come.

Odeio o que não vejo. Se pudera,
    Vel-o, grato o não vira.
Se m'o mostrára um quadro, ou o virára
    Não tenho o que não tenho.
O que o Destino manda, saiba-o elle.
    A ignorancia me basta.

122

Hora a hora não dura a face antiga
Dos repetidos seres, e hora a hora,
    Pensando, envelhecemos.
Tudo passa ignorado, e o que, sabido,
Fica, sabe que ignora, porém nada
    Torna, sciente ou nescio.
Pares, assim, do que não somos pares,
Da hora incerta a chama agasalhemos
    Com concavas mãos frias.

123

Não torna atraz a negregada prole
    Regular de Saturno,
Nem magnos deuses implorados volvem
    Quem foi á luz que vemos.
Moramos, hospedes na vida, e usamos
    Um tempo do discurso,
Um breve amor, um sorriso breve, e um dia
    Saüdoso de todos.

I hate what I cannot see. Even if I could actually
    See it, I would prefer not to.
Even if they showed it to me in a painting, and I saw it,
    I still do not have what I do not have.
What Destiny ordains, only Destiny knows.
    Not knowing is enough for me.

122   [16 November 1923]

The former faces of our repeated selves last
Not even an hour, and with each hour,
    We age even as we think.
Everything that happens is an unknown, and anything known
That remains knows it does not know, and yet nothing,
    Wise or foolish, ever returns.
As the equals, then, of what we are not the equal,
Let us guard the flame of the uncertain hour
    Cupped in our cold hands.

123   [16 November 1923]

They do not return, the dark, unhappy
    Progeny of Saturn,
Nor do great gods, even if we beg them, restore
    The departed to the light we see.
We are merely guests in life, with time
    Only for a conversation,
A brief love, a brief smile, and a day
    Longing for all those things.

124

Cantos, risos e flores allumiem
　　Nosso mortal destino,
Para o ermo occultar fundo, nocturno
　　De nosso pensamento,
Curvado, já em vida, sob a idéa
　　Do plutonico gôzo,
Cônscio já da livida sperança
　　Do Chaos redivivo.

125

Se has de ser o que choras
Ter que ser, não o chores.
Se toda a mole immensa
Do mundo ser-te ha noite,
Aproveita este breve
Dia, e sem choro ou cura
Goza-o, contente por viveres
O pouco que te é dado.

126

O merecer e o receber não teem
Commum medida. Uma é a lei que deramos,
Outra a que os deuses deram. Merecemos
De um lado e do outro recebemos nem
Um lado é mais que o outro lado do outro.
Ignotas causas geram ignorados
Efeitos conhecidos. Entrevemos,
E a parte que do todo ao olhar nos cabe
Não reproduz o todo em menos, é
Parte diversa dele. No que vemos
Nada vemos do todo, e só o que vemos.

124

May songs, laughter, and flowers illumine
    Our mortal destiny,
And thus conceal the deep, nocturnal wilderness
    Of our thoughts,
Weighed down, even while we live, by the idea
    Of Plutonic pleasure,
Already conscious of the pale hope
    Of Chaos resurrected.

125

Since you must be what you weep
To have to be, do not weep.
Since the whole vast edifice
Of the world will turn to night,
Make the most of this brief
Day, and with no tears, no remedy,
Enjoy it, glad that you can live
The little that is given to you.

126

What we deserve and what we receive
Have no common measure. One is the law we ourselves made,
The other was made by the gods. We deserve
From one side and receive from the other, and one side
Is no more important than the other's other side.
Unknown causes generate unknown
Known effects. We merely catch a glimpse,
And the part of the whole that our gaze takes in
Does not reproduce a lesser version of that whole,
But is a diverse part of it. In what we see
We never see the whole, but only what we see.

127

Com que vida encherei os poucos breves
Dias que me são dados? Será minha
    A minha vida ou dada
    A outros ou a sombras?

Á sombra de nós mesmos quantos homens
Inconscientes nos sacrificamos,
    E um destino cumprimos
    Nem nosso nem alheio!

Porem nosso destino é o que fôr nosso,
Que nos deu a sorte, ou, alheio fado,
    Anonymo a um anonymo,
    Nos arrasta a corrente.

Ó deuses immortaes, saiba eu ao menos
Acceitar sem querel-o, sorridente,
    O curso aspero e duro
    Da strada permitida.

128

Não perscrutes o anonymo futuro,
Lydia; é egual o futuro perscrutado
Ao que não perscrutámos,
Quem o dá, o dá feito.

Disformes sonhos antecipam cousas
Que serão peores que os disformes sonhos.
No temor do futuro
Nos futuros mactamos.

127 [5 May 1925]

With what life will I fill the few brief
Days that have been given to me? Will
    My life be mine or given
    To others or to mere shadows?

Huddled beneath our own shadow, how many of us
Unwittingly sacrifice our lives,
    And fulfill a destiny that belongs
    Neither to us nor to another!

And yet our destiny is whatever befalls us,
Whatever was given to us by chance or by indifferent fate,
    As one anonymous being to another,
    We are swept along on the current.

O immortal gods, let me at least know
How to accept, unwillingly, but with a smile,
    The harsh, hard course
    Of the single permitted path.

128 [13 June 1925]

Do not scrutinize the anonymous future,
Lydia; the future, whether scrutinized or not,
Remains the same, for whoever
Gives it, gives it ready-made.

Distorted dreams anticipate things
Far worse than those same dreams.
Out of fear for the future,
We chisel other futures.

Saber vêr só até o horizonte
E o dia, memore da flôr hesterna
Mais que do melhor fructo
Que talvez não colhamos.

129

O tudo, que exclue só a nossa fé,
O anonymo destino indifferente
Ao que em nós pensa o que em nós sente,
Injusto porque é
Nem justo nem injusto no atro fundo
E a varia sorte, e o imperfeito mundo.

130

Morreste aqui no fim da primavera
Para symbolo eterno do que passa
Antes que alcance o que sonha e spera,
Ou o que spera sem querer sonhal-o
Ou o que, alumno antigo da desgraça,
Não spera ou sonha, e ancia alcançal-o.
Nada aprende do mundo o altivo spirito
Que consome em si mesmo o fogo e a luz
Da indivisivel ansia do Infinito.

131

No cyclo eterno das mudaveis cousas
Novo hynverno após novo outomno volve
Á differente terra
Com a mesma maneira.

Learn to see only as far as the horizon,
To see the day as a memento of yesterday's flower
Rather than of the finer fruit
We perhaps failed to pick.

129   [c. 13 June 1925]

The whole, which excludes only our faith,
The anonymous destiny indifferent
To what inside us thinks that which we feel,
And unjust because there is
Neither just nor unjust in the dark depths,
In inconstant fate, and the imperfect world.

130   [c. 13 June 1925]

You died here at the end of spring,
An eternal symbol of what happens
To one who dies without achieving his dreams and hopes,
Or what he hopes for without daring to dream
Or else, as a hardened student of misfortune,
For what he neither hopes nor dreams, yet yearns to achieve.
It learns nothing from the world, the lofty mind
That consumes within itself the fire and light
Of the indivisible yearning for the Infinite.

131   [24 November 1925]

In the eternal cycle of mutable things,
New winter after new autumn returns
To the different earth
Always in the same way.

Porém a mim nem me acha differente
Nem differente deixa-me, fechado
Na clausura maligna
Da indole indecisa.

Presa da pallida fatalidade
De não mudar-me, me infiel renovo
Aos propositos mudos
Morituros e infindos.

132
Sem clepsydra ou relogio o tempo escorre
E nós com elle, nada o arbitro scravo
      Pode contra o destino
Nem contra os deuses o mortal desejo.

Hoje, quaes servos com ausentes donos,
Na alheia casa, um dia sem o jugo,
      Bebamos e comamos.
Será para amanhã o que aconteça.

Tombae, mancebos, o vinho em nobre taça
E o braço nu com que o entornaes fique
      No lembrando olhar
Como uma agua que passa. Ah, vem o vinho!

Sim, heroes somos todos amanhã.
Hoje addiemos. E na erguida taça
      O roxo vinho espelhe
Depois—porque a noite nunca falta.

And yet it neither finds me different
Nor leaves me different, sealed
Inside the grim enclosure
Of my indecisive self.

Prey to the pallid fate
Of one who cannot change, I faithlessly renew
Old intentions: unspoken,
Moribund, undying.

132 [c. May 1926]

Without clepsydra or clock, time still flows on
And we along with it, not even that slavish arbiter
    Can outdo destiny
Nor mortal desire outdo the gods.

Today, like servants when their masters are away,
In someone else's house, a day free from the yoke,
    Let us drink and eat,
And let what happens tomorrow happen.

Pour the wine into the noble cup, lads,
And may the bare arm with which you pour it
    Linger in memory's eye
Like flowing water. Yes, bring on the wine!

Tomorrow, we will all be heroes.
But not today. And may the red wine
    In our raised cup mirror
What comes afterward—because night never fails to fall.

133

Não torna ao ramo a folha que o deixou,
Nem com seu mesmo pé se uma outra fórma.
O momento, que acaba ao começar
Este, morreu p'ra sempre.

Não me promette o incerto e vão futuro
Mais do que esta iterada experiencia
Da mortal sorte e a condição deserta
Das cousas e de mim.

Porisso, neste rio universal
De que sou, não uma onda, senão ondas,
Decorro inerte, sem pedido, nem
Deuses em quem o empregue.

134

Nem vã sperança nem, não menos vã,
Desesperança, Lydia, nos governa
        A consummanda vida.
Só spera ou desespera quem conhece
Que ha que sperar. Nós, no labento curso
        Do ser, só ignoramos.
Breves no triste goso desfolhamos
Rosas. Mais breves que nós fingem legar
        A comparada vida.

135

Fructos, dão-os as arvores que vivem,
Não a illudida mente, que só se orna
        Das flôres lividas
        Do intimo abysmo.

133 [28 September 1926, a.m. early]

The leaf does not return to the branch it left,
Nor with its stem does it take on another form.
The moment that ends when this one
Begins is dead and gone.

The uncertain, futile future promises me
Nothing but the repeated experience
Of my mortal fate and the desolate condition
Of things and of myself.

That is why, in this universal river,
In which I am not one wave but many,
I drift, inert, without the right to plead,
Nor any gods to whom I might appeal.

134 [28 September 1926, a.m. early]

Neither vain hope nor no less vain
Despair, Lydia, governs
    Our all-consuming life.
Only he who knows there is something to hope for
Hopes or despairs. Poised on the slippery slope
    Of existence, all we know is nothing.
We, brief souls, take melancholy pleasure in plucking
The petals from roses. They, briefer still, appear to promise
    An equally brief life.

135 [6 December 1926]

Fruit is borne only by the living trees,
Not the deluded mind that merely adorns itself
    With pale flowers
    From its inner abyss.

Quantos reinos nas mentes e nas cousas
Te não talhaste imaginario! Tantos,
    Sem ter perdeste,
    Antedeposto.

Ah, contra o adverso muito nada proprio
E unico vences, fruste. A vida é invia.
    Abdica e sê
    Rei só de ti.

136

Goso sonhado é goso, inda que em sonho.
Nós o que nos suppomos nos fazemos,
    Se com attenta mente
    Resistirmos em crel-o.

Não, pois, meu modo de pensar nas coisas,
Nos seres e no Fado me censures.
    Para mim crio tanto
    Quanto para mim crio.

Fóra de mim, alheio ao em que penso,
O fado cumpre-se. Porém eu me cumpro
    Segundo o ambito breve
    Do que por meu me é dado.

137

O relogio de sol partido marca
Do mesmo modo que o inteiro o lapso
    Da mesma hora perdida ...
O mesmo goso com que esqueço, ou o creio,

How many imaginary kingdoms did you once carve
Out of thoughts and things! How many did you lose
      Without ever having had them,
      Unthroned before you began.

Ah, from your adversary you will win nothing
Uniquely, fleetingly your own. Life knows no paths.
      Abdicate and be
      King of yourself.

136   [30 January 1927]
Dreamed pleasure is still pleasure even if dreamed.
We become what we imagine ourselves to be,
      If, with an attentive mind,
      We insist on believing it.

Do not, therefore, criticize my way of thinking
Of things and beings and Fate.
      What I create for myself
      I create only for myself.

Outside of me, oblivious to what I may think,
Fate fulfills itself. Meanwhile, I fulfill myself
      Within the brief ambit
      Given to me as mine.

137   [30 January 1927]
Both the broken and the unbroken sundial
Mark in the same way the passing
      Of the same lost hour …
The same pleasure with which I forget, or think I do,

A vida, findo, me a mim mesmo mostra
    Mais fatal e mortal,
Para onde quer que siga a certa noite
    Quer ou não a vejamos.

138
Solemne passa sobre a fertil terra
A branca, inutil nuvem fugidia,
Que um negro instante de entre os campos ergue
    Um sopro arrefecido.

Tal me alta na alma a lenta idéa voa
E me ennegrece a mente, mas já torno,
Como a si mesmo o mesmo campo, ao dia
    Superficie da vida.

139
Atraz não torna, nem, como Orpheu, volta
    Sua face, Saturno.
Sua severa fronte reconhece
    Só o lugar do futuro.
Não temos mais de certo que o instante
    Em que o pensamos certo.
Não o pensemos, pois, mas o façamos
    Certo sem pensamento.

140
Emquanto eu vir o sol luzir nas folhas
E sentir toda a briza nos cabellos
    Não quererei mais nada.

About fast-fading life reveals me to myself
As more fated and more mortal,
Set on the path of wherever the inevitable night will take us
Whether we choose to see it or not.

138   [31 May 1927]

The fleeting, vain, white cloud
Passes solemnly over the fertile earth,
And for a dark moment there rises up from the fields
A cooler breeze.

Just as an illusory idea sometimes hovers over my soul,
Darkening my mind, until I return,
As that same field does to itself, to the day,
To the surface of life.

139   [31 May 1927]

Saturn does not turn back, nor, like Orpheus,
Does he look behind him.
His stern face recognizes
Only the future.
All we have of certainty is the instant
When we think it certain.
Therefore, let us not think, but, rather,
Unthinking, make it certain.

140   [16 June 1927]

As long as I can see the sun shining on the leaves
And feel the breeze in my hair
I will want for nothing more.

Que me pode o Destino conceder
Melhor que o lapso sensual da vida
        Entre ignorancias destas?

Pomos a duvida onde ha rosas. Damos
Quasi tudo do sentido a entendel-o
        E ignoramos, pensantes.
Extranha a nós a natureza extensa
Campos ondula, flores abre, fructos
        Córa, e a morte chega.

Terei razão, se a alguem razão é dada,
Quando me a morte conturbar a mente
        E já não veja mais
Que á razão de saber porque vivemos
Nós nem a achamos nem achar se deve,
        Impropicia e profunda.

Sabio deveras o que não procura,
Que, procurando, achára o abysmo em tudo
        E a duvida em si-mesmo.

141
Aqui, dizeis, na cova a que me chego,
Não stá quem eu amei. Olhar nem falla
        Se escondem nesta leiva.
Ah, mas olhos e bocca aqui se escondem!
Mãos apertei, não alma, e aqui morrem.
        Homem, um corpo chóro.

What better thing can Destiny grant me
Than this, life's slow sensual slide
    In among such ignorances?

Let us plant our doubts where there are roses. Let us give
Almost everything the meaning we feel it has, but which
    On reflection, we do not know.
All of vast nature is a stranger to us:
Fields ripple, flowers open, fruits
    Ripen, and death arrives.

I will be right, if anyone is ever right,
When death befuddles my mind
    And I see only
That we should not know why we live
Nor should we seek to know the reason,
    Impropitious and profound.

Wise indeed is he who does not seek, because,
In seeking, he will find the abyss that exists in all things
    And in himself only doubt.

141 [6 July 1927]

Here, you say, in the grave I am visiting,
Lies not the one I loved. Neither eyes nor words
    Are hidden beneath this mound.
Ah, but eyes and mouth do lie hidden here!
I clasped a hand, not a soul, and here it lies dead.
    It is for a man, a body, I weep.

142

Lenta, descança a onda que a maré deixa.
Pesada cede. Tudo é socegado.
    Só o que é de homem se ouve.
    Cresce o luar ausente.

Nesta hora, Lydia ou Neera ou Chloé,
Qualquer de vós me é extranha, que me inclino
    Só para o vão segredo
    Dicto pela incerteza.

Tomo nas mãos, como caveira, ou chave,
De superfluo sepulchro, meu destino,
    E ignaro o aborreço
    Sem coração que o sinta.

143

Quantos gosam o goso de gosar
Sem que gosem o goso; e o dividem
    Entre elles e o verem
    Os outros que elles gosam.

Ah, Lydia, os trajos do gosar omitte,
Que o goso é um, se é nosso, nem o damos
    Aos outros como premio
    De verem nosso goso.

Cada um é elle só, e se com outros
Gosa, dos outros gose, não para elles.
    Apprende o que te ensina
    Teu corpo, teu limite.

142

The slow wave left by the tide first rests,
Then heavily withdraws. All is quiet.
    Only human things can be heard.
    The absent moonlight grows.

At this hour, Lydia or Neaira or Chloe,
All of you are strangers to me, for I am listening
    Only for the futile secret
    Uttered by uncertainty.

In my hands, as if it were a skull, or the key
To some superfluous tomb, I hold my destiny,
    And fool that I am, I loathe it,
    Having no heart with which to feel it.

143

How many enjoy the enjoyment of enjoying themselves
Without actually enjoying their enjoyment; and share it
    Among themselves, that and being seen by others
    To be enjoying themselves.

Ah, Lydia, discard all the trappings of enjoyment,
Because enjoyment is ours alone and should not be given
    To others like a reward
    For seeing our enjoyment.

We are each of us ourselves alone, and if you enjoy yourself
With others, then enjoy them, don't do their enjoying for them.
    Learn what your body,
    Your boundary, teaches you.

144

Floresce em ti, ó magna terra, em cores
A varia primavera, e o verão vasto,
    E os campos são de alegres.

Mas dorme em cada campo o outomno d'elle
O hynverno cresce com as folhas verdes
    Tudo será esquecido.

145

Toda visão da crença se acompanha,
Toda crença da acção; e a acção se perde,
    Agua em agua entre tudo.
Conhece-te, se podes. Se não podes
Conhece que não podes. Saber sabe.
    Sê teu. Não dês nem speres.

146

O somno é bom pois dispertamos d'elle
Para saber que é bom. Se a morte é somno
    Dispertaremos d'ella;
    Se não, e não é somno,

Com quanto em nós é nosso a refusemos
Emquanto em nossos corpos condemnados
    Dura, do carcereiro,
    A licença indecisa.

Lydia, a vida mais vil antes que a morte,
Que desconheço, quero; e as flores colho
    Que te entrego, votivas
    De um pequeno destino.

144 [9 October 1927]

Ah, in you, great earth, the bustling spring
And the vast summer both burst into colorful bloom,
    And the fields are happy.

But sleeping in every field is each field's autumn,
And the winter grows along with the green leaves,
    And all will be forgotten.

145 [19 October 1927]

Any vision of belief comes in company,
Every belief involves action, and all action is lost,
    Like water in water.
Know yourself, if you can. If you can't,
Know that you can't. Knowing knows.
    Be yours alone. Neither give nor hope.

146 [19 November 1927]

Sleep is good because we wake from it
And know that it is good. If death is sleep
    We will wake from that too;
    If not, it is not sleep.

Let us reject it then with all our might
For as long as over our condemned bodies
    There hangs the jailer's
    Indecisive verdict.

Lydia, better the basest of lives than death,
Which I do not wish to know, and the flowers I pick
    For you are the votive offerings
    Of one small destiny.

147

Cada momento que a um prazer não voto
Perco, nem curo se o prazer me é dado;
　　　Porque o sonho de um goso
　　　No goso não é sonho.

148

Cada um é um mundo; e como em cada fonte
Uma deidade vela, em cada homem
　　　Porque não há de haver
　　　Um deus só de elle homem?

149

Pensa quantos, no ardor da jovem ida,
Um destino parou; quantos, obtendo
　　　A meta, a descobriram
　　　Antes que o ardor quizesse.

Não speres nem consigas; enche a taça
E abdica: tudo é natural e extranho.
　　　Nem justos nem injustos
　　　São os Deuses, senão outros.

O conseguido é dado; tudo é imposto.
Prazer ou magua, são qual sol ou chuva,
　　　Dados, ora aos desejos
　　　Ora ao […]

147 [1927–1928]

Each moment not devoted to some pleasure
Is a moment lost, nor does it count if the pleasure is a gift;
    Because a pleasure dreamt,
    While it lasts, is not a dream.

148 [1927–1928]

Each of us is a world; and just as a deity
Watches over every spring, why, for each man,
    Should there not be
    A god unique to him?

149 [3 January 1928]

Think how many destinies, in the ardor of lost youth,
Are stopped and stalled; how many, finding
    A goal, discovered it before
    That same ardor so chose.

Neither hope nor achieve; fill your cup
And abdicate: all is both natural and strange.
    The Gods are neither just
    Nor unjust, they are simply other.

What you achieve is given; everything is imposed.
Pleasure or pain are like the sun or the rain,
    Granted now to desires
    Now to […]

RICARDO REIS

20/2/28. Ricardo Reis.
----

1   Pesa o decreto atroz do fim certeiro
     Pesa e sentença egual do algoz igusto
     Em cada cerviz nossa., E entrudo e riem.
     Felizes, porque nelles (em elles) pensa e sente
     A vida, que não elles.

3   Se a sciencia é vida, sabio é só o nescio.
     Quem pouco differença entre a mente interna
     Do homem e dos brutos? Sús! Deixae
     ...... os moribundos!
     De rosas, inda que de falsas, tecam
2   Capellas veres. Breve o ver é o
     Que lhes é dado, e por misericordia
     ...... Breve nem vê sentido.

     Vou dormir, dormir, dormir,
     Vou dormir sem ...... dispertar,
     Mas não dormir sem sentir
     Que stou dormindo e sonhar.

     Não a insciencia e o ......,
     Mas tambem strellas a abrir
     Olhos em cujo olhar me eleva,
     Que stou sonhando e dormir.

     Vou dormir, vou dispertar
     Para outra vida em redor,

RICARDO REIS

Odes 150, 151, and 153

26/4/28

RICARDO REIS

p.113

p.112

Odes 155, 156, and 157

150

Pese a sentença egual da ignota morte
Em cada breve corpo, é entrudo e riem,
Felizes, porque em elles pensa e sente
    A vida, que não elles.

De rosas, inda que de falsas, teçam
Capellas veras. Scasso, curto é o spaço
Que lhes é dado, e por bom caso em todos
    Breve nem vão sentido.

Se a sciencia é vida, sabio é só o nescio.
Quam pouco differença a mente interna
Do homem da dos brutos! Sús! Leixae
    Viver os moribundos!

151

Nirvâna
Vou dormir, dormir, dormir,
Vou dormir sem dispertar,
Mas não dormir sem sentir
Que stou dormindo a sonhar.

Não a insciencia e só treva
Mas tambem strellas a abrir
Olhos cujo olhar me enleva,
Que stou sonhando a dormir.

Stellar, negra inexistencia
Em que subsiste de meu
Só uma abstracta insciencia
Uma com strellas e céu.

150

Despite the same obscure death sentence hanging over
Each brief body, it's carnival-time and they laugh,
Happy, because all their thinking and feeling is done,
    Not by them, but by life.

Let them then weave real garlands out of roses,
Even if they're fake roses. However scant and brief
Their allotted space, they have the good fortune
    Not to feel that brevity.

If knowledge is life, then only the fool is wise.
How little the inner mind of a man differs
From that of a beast! So, hush now, and let
    The dying live!

151

Nirvana

I'm going to sleep, sleep, sleep,
I'm going to sleep and not wake up,
But I won't sleep without feeling
That I'm sleeping and dreaming.

It isn't all ignorance and darkness,
It is also stars opening
Eyes whose gaze delights me,
For I'm dreaming and sleeping.

A starry, black inexistence
In which all that remains of me
Is an abstract ignorance,
One with stars and sky.

152

Dois é o prazer: gosar e o gosal-o.
Ao nescio elege o parvo, o sabio ao certo.
    E o egual fado é diverso.
Na taça que ergo, rodo, e vejo, as bolhas
Incluo no que sinto, e ao prazer bebo
    Mais que stá no gosto.

153

Doce é o fructo á vista, e á boca amaro,
Breve é a vida ao tempo e longa á alma.
    A arte, com que todos
—Ora sem saber virando os copos idos,
Ora, enchendo-os, cientes—nos ousamos,
    Chegada a morte, despir.

154

Concentra-te, e serás sereno e forte;
Mas concentra-te fóra de ti mesmo.
Não sê mais para ti que o pedestal
No qual ergas a statua do teu ser.
Tudo mais empobrece, porque é pobre.

155

Ingloria é a vida, e inglorio o conhecal-a.
Quantos, se pensam, já se desconhecem
    Os que se conheceram!
A cada hora se muda não só a hora
Mas o que se vê nella, e a vida passa
    Entre viver e ser.

152

Pleasure is twofold: there is pleasure and enjoying the pleasure.
The fool chooses foolishly, the wise man chooses wisely.
     And their shared fate is different.
In the cup I raise and swirl and contemplate, I include
The bubbles in what I feel, and the pleasure of drinking
     Goes beyond the pleasure of the taste.

153

Fruit is sweet to the eye and bitter to the mouth,
Life is short in time and long in the soul.
     The art that all of us
—Now unwittingly overturning empty cups,
Now knowingly filling them—finally dare,
     When death arrives, to cast off.

154

Focus, and you will be serene and strong;
But focus yourself outside of yourself.
Be no more than the pedestal on which
You erect the statue of your being.
Anything else impoverishes, because it is poor.

155

Life is inglorious, and knowing equally inglorious.
How many, if they stop to think, do not recognize themselves,
     If they ever did!
With every hour, not only the hour changes
But what we see in it too, and life passes
     Between living and existing.

156

Nos altos ramos de arvores frondosas
O vento faz um rumor frio e alto.
Nesta floresta, em este som me perco
    E sósinho medito.

Assim no mundo, acima do que sinto,
Um vento faz a vida, e a deixa, e a toma,
E nada tem sentido—nem a alma
    Com que penso sósinho.

157

O annel dado ao mendigo é injuria, e a sorte
Dada a quem pensa é infamia, que quem pensa
    Quer verdade, e não sorte.

Como um mendigo a quem é dado o nome
De rei, não come d'elle, mas do prato
    Do rei, minha sperança
Da razão que ha em tel-a se alimenta
    E não do que deseja.

158

Tudo que cessa é morte, e a morte é nossa
Se é para nós que cessa. Aquelle arbusto
    Fenece, e vae com elle
    Parte da minha vida.

Em tudo quanto olhei fiquei em parte.
Com tudo quanto vi, se passa, passo,
    Nem distingue a memoria
    Do que vi do que fui.

156 [26 April 1928]

In the high branches of the leafy trees
The wind is making a cold, high, murmur.
In this forest, I lose myself in the sound
    And alone I meditate.

So in the world, high above my feelings,
A wind blows through life, lifting it up then leaving it,
And nothing has any meaning—not even the soul
    With which I meditate alone.

157 [26 April 1928]

The ring given to a beggar is an insult, just as a fate
Given to a thinking man is a dishonor, for any thinking person
    Wants the truth, not fate.

Just as a beggar given the name of a king
Dines not off the king's name, but off
    The king's plate, so my hope
Nourishes itself on the reason for that hope
    Not on what it desires.

158 [7 June 1928]

Everything that ceases is death, and if it ceases for us
Then that is our death. That bush over there
    Is dying, and with it dies
    A small part of my life.

For a part of me remains in everything I ever looked at,
And if something I have seen dies, then I die too,
    And memory makes no distinction
    Between what I saw and what I was.

159

Tarda o verão. No campo tributario
Da nossa sprança, não ha sol bastante,
Nem se speravam as que veem, chuvas
    Na estação, deslocadas.

Meu vão conhecimento do que vejo
Com o que é falso se contenta, ou muito,
Ou pouco dado á conclusão facticia
    Do moribundo tudo.

160

A cada qual, como a statura, cabe
    A justiça: uns faz altos
    A sorte, outros felizes.
Nada é premio: succede o que acontece.
    Nada, Lydia, devemos
    Ao fado, senão tel-o.

161

Nem da herva humilde se o Destino esquece.
    Seiva a lei o que vive.
De sua natureza murcham rosas
    E prazeres se acabam.
Quem nos conhece, amigo, taes quaes fomos?
    Nem nós nos conhecemos.

162

Quem diz ao dia, Dura! e á treva, Acaba!
    E a si não diz, Não digas!
Sentinellas absurdas, vigilamos,
    Inscios dos contendentes.

159 [7 June 1928]

Summer is late arriving. In the tributary land
Of our hope, there is not enough sun,
Nor did anyone expect the rains to come
        So out of place and out of season.

My futile knowledge of what I see
Contents itself with what is false, and happily
Or not reaches the factitious conclusion
        That all is dying.

160 [20 November 1928]

As with our height or lack of it, fate deals out
        Justice: some are raised up,
        Others are made happy.
There are no prizes: what happens happens.
        Nothing, Lydia, do we owe
        To fate, except to have it.

161 [20 November 1928]

Destiny forgets not even the humble blade of grass.
        Sap, the law of life.
It is the nature of roses and pleasures
        To wither away and die.
Who, my friend, can recall us just as we once were?
        Not even we could do that.

162 [21 November 1928]

Like someone saying to the day, Last! and to the darkness, End!
        But failing to tell himself, Hush now!
We keep watch, absurd sentinels ignorant
        Of who our enemies are.

Uns com o frio, outros a um ar bom, guardam
O posto e a propria insciencia.

163

Negue-me tudo a sorte, salvo vel-a,
Que eu, stoico sem dureza,
Na sentença gravada do Destino
Quero gosar as lettras.

164

Sê lanterna, sê luz com vidro em torno,
Porém o calor guarda.
Não poderão os ventos oppressivos
Apagar tua luz;
Nem teu calor, disperso, irá ser frio
No inutil infinito.

165

Áquelle que, constante, nada spera
Não pode negar Jove; nem para elle
Murcham as frageis flores
Que nunca sperou vêr.

Consiste a força do animo em não tel-a
Para os alacres fins da fantasia,
Mas em saber conter-se
Nos limites d [...]

Some wait in the cold, others in the soft air, guarding
    Their post and their own ignorance.

163   [21 November 1928]
Fate, deny me anything but the chance to view my fate,
    For, lax stoic that I am,
On the sentence engraved by Destiny I wish
    Simply to enjoy the lettering.

164   [3 March 1929]
Be a lantern, be a light surrounded by glass
    To keep the warmth in.
No buffeting winds will be strong enough
    To extinguish your light;
Nor will your warmth, once dispersed, grow cold
    In futile infinity.

165   [21 March 1929]
Jove cannot deny the constant man
Who hopes for nothing, nor, for him,
    Do the fragile flowers wither,
    Flowers he never hoped to see.

True strength of mind means not wasting it
On imagination's blithe ambitions,
    But knowing how to keep oneself
    Within the bounds of […]

166

Se recordo quem fui, outrem me vejo,
E o passado, presente da lembrança
    Sinto-me como em sonho
    Porem sòmente em sonho.

E a saüdade que me afflige a mente
Não é de mim nem do passado visto,
    Senão de quem habito
    Por traz dos olhos cegos.

Nada, senão o instante, me conhece.
Minha mesma lembrança é nada, e sinto
    Quem sou e os que fui
    São sonhos differentes.

167

No breve numero de doze mezes
O anno passa, breves são os annos,
    Poucos a vida dura.
Que são doze ou sessenta na floresta
Dos numeros, e quanto pouco falta
    Para o fim do futuro!
Dois terços já, tão rapido, do curso
Dado em declive deixo, e invito apresso
    O moribundo passo.

168

Não sei de quem recordo meu passado
Que outrem fui quando o fui, nem se conheço
Como sentindo com minha alma aquella
    Alma que a sentir lembro.

166

If I recall who I was, I see a stranger,
And the past as memory's present,
    I feel as if I existed in a dream,
    But only in a dream.

And the yearning that afflicts my mind
Is not for myself or for that glimpsed past,
    But for the person I inhabit
    Behind unseeing eyes.

Nothing knows me, only the moment.
Even my own memory is nothing, and I feel
    That who I am and those I was
    Are merely different dreams.

167

[18 June 1930]

In only a brief twelve months
The year passes, the years are brief,
    Life itself is short-lived.
And what is twelve or sixty in the forest
Of numbers, and how little time remains
    Before the future reaches its end!
Already two thirds of my journey have sped past me
Down the downward slope, and, reluctantly,
    I hasten on my dying steps.

168

[2 July 1930]

Whose past it is that I recall I do not know,
Nor who I was when I was that person, nor do I
Know myself, as if, with my own soul, I feel
    That other soul only in recollection.

De dia a outro nos desamparamos.
Nada de verdadeiro a nós nos une.
Somos quem somos, e quem fomos foi
    Coisa vista por dentro.

169

Quem fui é externo a mim. Se lembro, vejo;
E ver é ser alheio. Meu passado
    Só por visão relembro.
Aquillo mesmo que senti me é claro.
Alheia é a alma antiga; o que me sinto
    Chegou hoje à estalagem.
Quem pode conhecer, entre tanto erro
De modos de sentir-se, a exacta fórma
    Que tem para comsigo?

170

O que sentimos, não o que é sentido,
É o que temos. Claro, o inverno estreita.
    Como á sorte o acolhamos.
Haja inverno na terra, não na mente,
E, amor a amor, ou livro a livro, amemos
    Nossa lareira breve.

171

Debil no vicio, debil na virtude
A humanidade debil, nem na furia
    Conhece mais que a norma.
Pares e differentes nos regemos
Por uma norma propria, e inda que dura,
    Será á liberdade.

We unhouse ourselves from one day to the next,
And nothing real and true binds us to us.
We are who we are, and the person we were
    Merely a thing glimpsed inside us.

169   [2 July 1930]

Who I was lies outside of me. If I remember, I see;
And to see is to be outside. I recollect
    My past solely as a vision.
Only what I actually felt remains clear to me.
My former soul a stranger; for who I now am
    Arrived at the inn only today.
Given all the mistaken ways we have of feeling who we are,
Who can possibly know the exact form our self
    Takes on for us?

170   [8 July 1930]

What we feel, not what is felt,
Is all we have. Yes, the winter tightens its grip.
    Let us welcome it as we do our fate.
Let there be winter on the earth, not in the mind,
And from love to love, or book to book, let us love
    This our brief fireside.

171   [9 July 1930]

Weak in vice, weak in virtue,
Weak humanity, even when enraged,
    Knows only the norm.
Whether the same or different we are ruled
By our own norm, and as long as it lasts,
    It will mean freedom.

Ser livre é ser a propria imposta norma
Egual a todos, salvo no amplo e duro
        Mando e uso de si mesmo.

172
Não mais pensada que a dos mudos brutos
Se fada a humana vida. Quem destina
        Mais que os gados nos campos
        O fim do seu destino?

173
Não sei se é amor que tens, ou amor que finges,
O que me dás. Dás-m'o. Tanto me baste.
        Já que o não sou por tempo,
        Seja eu jovem por erro.

Pouco os Deuses nos dão, e o pouco é falso.
Porém, se o dão, falso que seja, a dadiva
        É verdadeira. Acceito,
        E a te crer me resigno.

174
Quer pouco: terás tudo.
Quer nada: serás livre.
O mesmo amor que tenham
Por nós, quer-nos, opprime-nos.

175
Não só quem nos odía ou nos inveja
Nos limita e opprime; quem nos ama
        Não menos nos limita.

To be free is to be the same self-imposed norm
Identical to all others, except in the harsh, all-encompassing
    Way in which we apply it to ourself.

172   [c. July 1930]
Human life is no more considered than that
Of dumb beasts. Which of us has any more control
    Over how our life ends
    Than do the cattle in the fields?

173   [12 September 1930]
I don't know if what you feel for me is real love
Or pretend love. But give it to me anyway. It will do.
    Since I'm no longer young in years
    Let me be young in my mistakes.

The Gods give us so little, and the little they give is false.
However, since they do give it, false though it be,
    The gift is genuine. I accept,
    And resign myself to believing you.

174   [1 November 1930]
Want little: you will have everything.
Want nothing: you will be free.
The very love they hold
For us binds us, oppresses us.

175   [1 November 1930]
Not only those who hate or envy us
Limit and oppress us; those who love us
    Limit us no less.

Que os Deuses me concedam que, despido
De affectos, tenha a fria liberdade
    Dos pincaros sem nada.
Quem quer pouco, tem tudo; quem quer nada
É livre; quem não tem, e não deseja,
    Homem, é egual aos deuses.

176

Não quero, Chloe, teu amor, que opprime
Porque me exige amor. Quero ser livre.

A esperança é um dever do sentimento.

177

Nunca a alheia vontade, inda que grata,
Cumpras por propria. Manda no que fazes,
    Nem de ti mesmo servo.
Ninguem te dá quem és. Nada te mude.
Teu intimo destino involuntario
    Cumpre alto. Sê teu filho.

178

No mundo, só commigo, me deixaram
    Os Deuses que dispõem.
Não posso contra elles: o que deram
    Acceito sem mais nada.
Assim o trigo baixa ao vento, e, quando
    O vento cessa, ergue-se.

May the Gods grant me that, stripped
Of all affections, I may enjoy the cold freedom
        Of the bare mountain peaks.
He who wants little, has everything; he who wants nothing
Is free; he who has nothing and wants nothing
        Is equal to the Gods.

176   [1 November 1930]
I don't want your love, Chloe, it's too oppressive,
Because it demands that I love too. And I want to be free.

Hope is a duty imposed by sentiment.

177   [19 November 1930]
Never do another person's bidding—however pleasing—
As if it were yours. Take charge of what you do,
        Do not be a slave even to yourself.
No one gives you who you are. Change nothing about you.
Fulfill to the maximum your own involuntary
        Destiny. Be your own child.

178   [19 November 1930
The Gods who decide all things, set me down
        In the world, alone with myself.
I cannot rebel against them: what they gave
        I willingly accept.
Just as the wheat bends in the wind and, when
        The wind drops, rises again.

179

A mim, Chloe, donzella, que nada fui, nem lhes era,
Ás sombras povoadas os grandes deuses deram.
Assim querem deuses. Fiz só duas vezes septe annos.
Onde fui me não lembram, nem paes, nem gado, nem nada.

180

Quero dos deuses só que me não lembrem.
Serei livre—sem dita nem desdita,
　　Como o vento que é a vida
　　Do ar que não é nada.

O odio e o amor eguaes nos buscam; ambos,
Cada um com seu modo, nos opprimem.
　　Só quem deuses concedem
　　Nada, tem liberdade.

181

Ser feliz é um jugo, e o ser grande
É uma servidão: tudo repugno
　　Salvo esta majestade.

182

Os deuses e os Messias que são deuses
Passam, e os sonhos vãos que são Messias.
　　A terra muda dura.
Nem deuses, nem Messias, nem idéas
Me trazem rosas. Minhas são se as tenho.
　　Se as tenho, que mais quero?

179 [c. 1930]

To me, fair Chloe—I who was nothing, nor anything to them—
The gods gave the crowded shades.
That is what gods want. I was only twice seven years old.
Where I passed no one remembers, neither parents, nor cattle,
    nothing.

180 [c. 1930]

All I want of the gods is for them to forget about me.
I will be free then—neither happy nor unhappy,
    Like the wind that is the life
    Of the air, which is nothing at all.

Hatred and love both equally seek us out,
Each in its own way an oppressor.
    Only those to whom the gods
    Grant nothing are truly free.

181 [c. 1930]

Happiness is a yoke, and greatness
A form of servitude: I reject everything
    Except this majestic state.

182 [8 February 1931]

The gods and those Messiahs who are gods all pass,
As do the vain dreams that are also Messiahs.
    The dumb earth endures.
Neither gods, nor Messiahs, nor ideas
Bring me roses. They are mine if I have them.
    And if I have them, why want more?

183

Do que quero renego, si o querel-o
Me pesa na vontade. Nada que haja
     Val que lhe concedamos
     Uma attenção que doa.
Meu balde exponho á chuva, por ter agua.
Minha vontade, assim, ao mundo exponho.
     Nem quero mais que o dado
     Ou que o tido desejo.

184

Quem és, não o serás, que o tempo e a sorte
     Te mudarão em outro.
Para quê pois em seres te empenhares
     O que não serás tu?
Teu é o que és, teu o que tens, de quem
     É o que outro tiveres?

185

Breve o dia, breve o anno, breve tudo.
     Não tarda nada sermos.
Isto, pensado, me de a mente absorve
     Todos mais pensamentos.
O mesmo breve ser da magua pesa-me,
     Que, inda que dor, é vida.

186

Domina ou cala. Não te percas, dando
     Aquillo que não tens.
Que val o Cesar que serias? Gosa
     Bastar-te o pouco que és.

183 [14 March 1931]

I reject what I want, if the wanting
Weighs on my will. Nothing is worth
　　Our giving it an attention
　　That brings us only grief.
I leave my bucket out in the rain to collect water.
Likewise, I leave my will out in the world,
　　I want only what is given
　　And desire only what I have.

184 [22 September 1931]

Who you are now, you will not be, for time and fate
　　Will change you into another.
Why then strive so hard at being someone
　　Who will not be you?
What you are is yours, what you have is yours,
　　What then do you need of anyone else's?

185 [27 September 1931]

Brief the day, brief the year, brief everything.
　　Soon we, too, will be nothing.
When I think this, it absorbs all other
　　Thoughts in my head.
Even the most ephemeral of griefs weighs on me,
　　For, though it is pain, it is life.

186 [27 September 1931]

Take control or be silent. Don't lose yourself
　　By giving what you do not have.
Of what value is the Caesar you could be? Enjoy
　　Making do with the little you are.

Melhor te acolhe a vil choupana dada
    Que o palacio devido.

187

Tudo, desde ermos astros afastados
    A nós, nos dá o mundo.
E a tudo, alheios, nos acrescentamos,
    Pensando e interpretando.
A proxima herva a que a mão chega basta,
    O que há é o melhor.

188

Ninguem, na vasta selva religiosa,
Do mundo inumeravel, finalmente
    Vê o deus que conhece.
Só o que a brisa traz se ouve na brisa.
O que pensamos, seja amor ou deuses,
    Passa, porque passamos.

189

Outros com lyras ou com harpas narram,
    Eu com meu pensamento.
Que, por meio de musica, acham nada
    Se acham só o que sentem.
Mais pesam as palavras que, medidas,
    Dizem que o mundo existe.

190

Se a cada coisa que ha um deus compete,
Porque não haverá de mim um deus?
    Porque o não serei eu?

Better to go home to the lowly shack you were given
        Than to the palace that is your due.

187   [10 December 1931]
Everything, from the distant, barren stars to us,
        Is a gift from the world.
And we, strangers, add to that everything
        By thinking and interpreting.
The nearest weed our hand can pluck suffices,
        What is is always the best.

188   [10 December 1931]
No one, in the vast religious jungle
Of the uncountable world, ever finally
        Sees the god he knows.
In the wind we hear only what the wind brings.
What we think, whether it be love or gods,
        Passes because we pass.

189   [c. 10 December 1931]
Others tell their stories with lyres or harps,
        I with my thoughts.
But if, through music, they find only their feelings,
        They find nothing.
The measured words that say the world exists
        Have more weight.

190   [c. 16 December 1931]
If there is a god for every single thing,
Why shouldn't there be a god for me?
        Why shouldn't I be a god?

É em mim que o deus anima porque eu sinto.
O mundo externo claramente vejo—
    Coisas, homens, sem alma.

191

No magno dia até os sons são claros.
Pelo repouso do amplo campo tardam.
    Múrmura, a brisa cala.
Quizera, como os sons, nascer das cousas
Mas não ser d'ellas, consequência alada
    Com o real em baixo.

192

Como este infante que alourado dorme
    Fui. Hoje sei que ha morte.
Lydia, não haja taça por encher
    Nem amor que nos tarde.
Qualquer que seja o amor ou a taça, breve
    Cegamos. Teme e despe-te.

193

Azues os montes que estão longe param.
De elles a mim o vario campo à brisa,
Ou verde ou amarello ou variegado,
    Ondula incertamente.

Debil como uma haste de papoila
Me supporta o momento. Nada quero.
Que pesa o escrupulo do pensamento
    Na balança da vida?

It is in me that the god lives because I feel.
And I see the external world very clearly—
    Things, men, all without souls.

191   [c. 1931]

In the vast day, even the sounds are clear.
They linger over the quiet, ample countryside.
    The murmuring breeze falls silent.
I wish that I, like the sounds, could be born of things
But not be them, a mere wingèd consequence
    Hovering above the real.

192   [1931–1932]

Once I was like this fair-haired sleeping child.
    Today I know that death exists.
Lydia, let there be no cup to fill
    Nor love that comes too late.
Be it love or a cup, all will soon
    Go into darkness. Reverence it and stand naked.

193   [31 March 1932]

The mountains stand blue in the distance.
Between them and me, the motley windswept fields,
Sometimes green or yellow or variegated,
    Ripple uncertainly.

The moment, frail as the stem of a poppy,
Bears me up. I wish for nothing.
How much do the cares of the mind weigh
    In life's scales?

Como os campos, e vario, e como elles,
Exterior a mim, me entrego, filho
Ignorado do Chaos e da Noite
    Ás ferias em que existo.

194

Lydia, ignoramos. Somos extrangeiros
Onde quer que moremos. Tudo é alheio
    Nem falla lingua nossa.
Façamos de nós mesmos o retiro
Onde esconder-nos, timidos do insulto
    Do tumulto do mundo.
Que quer o amor mais que não ser dos outros?
Como um segredo dicto nos mysterios,
    Seja sacro por nosso.

195

Severo narro. Quanto sinto penso.
    Palavras são idéas.
Murmuro, o rio passa, e o som não passa,
    Que é nosso, não do rio.
Assim quizera o verso: meu e alheio
    E por mim mesmo lido.

196

Flores amo, não busco. Se apparecem
Me agrado ledo, que ha em buscar prazeres
    O desprazer da busca.
A vida seja como o sol, que é dado,
Nem arranquemos flores, que, arrancadas
    Não são nossas, mas mortas.

Like the motley fields, and, like them, outside myself,
I surrender entirely—I, the unacknowledged
Child of Chaos and of Night—
        To the brief holiday in which I exist.

194   [9 June 1932]
We know nothing, Lydia. We are strangers,
Regardless of where we live. Everything is foreign to us,
        Nothing even speaks our language.
Let us, then, make of ourselves the retreat we need
To hide away, cowed by the insulting
        Tumult of the world.
What more does love want than to belong to no one else?
Like a secret spoken of in the mysteries,
        Sacred because it is ours.

195   16 June 1932]
A rigorous narrator, whatever I feel I think.
        Words are ideas.
I murmur, the river passes, but not the sound,
        Which belongs to us, not the river.
This is how I want my poem to be: mine and another's,
        And read by me myself.

196   [6 June 1932]
I love flowers, but do not seek them out. If they appear
I am pleased and happy, but seeking out pleasures involves
        The displeasure of the search.
Let life be like the sun, which is given to us freely,
And let us not pluck flowers, for, once plucked,
        They are no longer ours, but dead.

197
No grande espaço de não haver nada
Que a noite finge, brilham mal os astros.
   Não ha lua, e ainda bem.
Neste momento, Lydia, considero
Tudo, e um frio que não ha me entra
   Na alma. Não existes.

198
Sereno aguarda o fim que pouco tarda.
Que é qualquer vida? Breves soes e somno.
   Quanto pensas emprega
   Em não muito pensares.

Ao nauta o mar obscuro é a rota clara.
Tu, na confusa solidão da vida,
   A ti mesmo te elege
   (Não sabes de outro) o porto.

199
Ninguem a outrem ama, senão que ama
O que de si ha nelle, ou é supposto.
Nada te pese que não te amem. Sentem-te
   Quem és, e és extrangeiro.
Cura de ser quem és, amem-te ou nunca.
Firme contigo, sofrerás avaro
   De penas […]

197 [c. 16 June 1932]

In the vast empty nothingness that the night
Pretends to be, the stars shine only dimly.
        No moon, but just as well,
For at this moment, Lydia, as I ponder
Everything, a non-existent cold enters
        My soul. And you do not exist.

198 [31 July 1932]

Wait serenely for the end that will not be long in coming.
What is a life, after all? A few brief suns and sleep.
        Use whatever you think
        To not think too much.

To the sailor the obscure sea offers a clear route.
You, in the confusing solitude of life,
        Must (since you know no other)
        choose your own harbor.

199 [10 August 1932]

No one loves anyone else, they love what they see
Or imagine they see of themselves in others.
Don't feel hurt because they do not love you. They sense
        What you are: a stranger.
Accept being who you are, let them love you or not.
Alone with yourself, you will become a miser
Of sorrows [...]

200

Já a belleza vejo com a mente
    E com pensar a amo.
    Assim me velho sinto.
Quem me dera o error restituido
    Com que a via tam perto
    Que o vel-a era sentil-a.

201

Ignora e spera. Quantos, por saberem,
Por não ser sciencia perdem a sperança.
    Quantos, porque souberam,
Não querem já saber mais nem recordam
Como esperar, da inutil sciencia ida—
    Servos libertos presos.

202

Que pesa que no pobre entendimento
Como extrangeiro peses? Sê quem és
    Nem cures de quem querem.
Algures onde ainda ha mundo, pensa em
Alguem comtigo, e os pastores são filhos
    Desse que te esperara.

203

Para quê complicar inutilmente,
Pensando, o que impensado existe? Nascem
    Hervas sem razão dada—
Para ellas olhos, não razões, tenhamos.
Como atravez de um rio as contemplemos.

200   [15 August 1932]

I now see beauty with my mind,
  Loving beauty in thought alone.
  This makes me feel old.
If only that youthful error could be restored,
  When beauty seemed so near,
  That to see it was to feel it.

201   [c. 15 August 1932]

Know nothing and hope. How many lose hope
When they see that knowing is not knowledge.
  How many, once they do know,
Wish to know no more of that defunct, futile knowledge,
And have even lost the ability to hope—
  Liberated captive serfs.

202   [c. 15 August 1932]

Of what importance is it if, in someone's feeble mind,
You are of as little import as a stranger? Be who you are
  And ignore what others want.
In some place where there are still people, imagine
Someone at your side, and that the shepherds are the children
  Of the person waiting for you.

203   [3 September 1932]

Why make what has not been thought
Unnecessarily complicated by thinking it? Weeds
  Grow for no reason—
Let us offer them eyes, not reasons.
Let us see them as if from across a river.

204

Vive sem horas. Quanto mede lesa,
    E quanto pensa mede.
Num fluido incerto nexo, como o rio
    Cujas ondas são elle,
Assim teus dias sê, e se te vires
    Passar, como a outrem, cala.

205

Nada fica de nada. Nada somos.
Um pouco ao sol e ao ar nos atrazamos
Da irrespiravel treva que nos pese
    Da humida terra imposta,
Cadaveres addiados que procriam.

Leis feitas, statuas vistas, odes findas—
Tudo tem cova sua. Se nós, carnes
A que um intimo sol dá sangue, temos
    Poente, porque não ellas?
Somos contos contando contos, nada.

206

Que mais que um ludo ou jogo é a extensa vida,
Em que nos distrahimos de outra coisa—
    Que coisa, não sabemos—;
Livres porque brincamos se jogamos,
Presos porque tem regras todo jogo;
    Quem somos? quem seremos?
Feliz o a quem surge a consciencia
Do jogo, mas não toda, e essa d'elle
    Em o saber perdel-a.

204 [8 September 1932]

Live without counting the hours. Anything measured offends,
    And every thinking thing measures.
May your days be a fluid, uncertain nexus, like the river
      Which is its own waves,
And should you happen to see yourself passing by
      Like a stranger, say nothing.

205 [28 September 1932]

Nothing of anything remains. We are nothing.
With a little sun and fresh air we postpone our encounter
With the unbreathable darkness imposed
      On us by the damp, heavy earth,
Corpses-in-waiting who procreate.

Laws made, statues seen, odes written—
All have their own grave. If we, flesh
Filled with blood by an inner sun, have
      Our own sunset, why should not they?
We are stories telling stories, we are nothing.

206 [27 October 1932]

What else but a sport or a game is a life spent
Avoiding thinking about something else—
      Quite what, we don't know—;
Free because we are having fun as we play,
Prisoners because every game has its rules;
      Who are we? Who will we be?
Happy the man who sees that it is all a game,
But not entirely, for if he knew this,
      He would lose.

207

Quanto faças, supremamente faze.
Mais vale, se a memoria é quanto temos,
        Lembrar muito que pouco.
E se o muito no pouco te é possível,
Mais ampla liberdade de lembrança
        Te tornará teu dono.

208

Rasteja molle pelos campos ermos
        O vento socegado.
Mais parece tremer de um tremor proprio,
        Que do vento, o que é herva.
E se as nuvens no céu, brancas e altas,
        Se movem, mais parecem
Que gira a terra rapida e ellas passam,
        Por muito altas, lentas.
Aqui neste socego dilatado
        Me esquecerei de tudo,
Nem hospede será do que conheço
        A vida que deslembro.
Assim meus dias seu decurso falso
        Gosarão verdadeiro.

209

Quero ignorado, e calmo
Por ignorado, e proprio
Por calmo, encher meus dias
De não querer mais d'elles.

Aos que a riqueza toca
O ouro irrita a pelle.

207 [27 February 1933]

Whatever you do, do it supremely.
If memory is all we have, better to remember
    A lot than a little.
And if you can recall a lot about the little
Then that greater freedom of recollection
    Will make you master of yourself.

208 [27 February 1933]

The quiet wind creeps very slowly across
    The deserted fields.
The grass seems to tremble, not in the wind,
    But of its own accord.
And if the high, white clouds in the sky move,
    It seems more as if they,
Those same high, slow clouds, were merely turning
    With the rapid turning of the earth.
Here in this ample quietude
    I will forget everything,
I will not even be a guest in what I know
    Of the life I am forgetting.
Thus my days will savor their false course
    As if it were true.

209 [2 March 1933]

Forgotten, and calm because forgotten,
and entirely my own self because I am calm,
I wish to fill my days with wanting
Nothing more from them.

The skin of those touched by wealth
Becomes irritated by the gold.

Aos que a fama bafeja
Embacia-se a vida.

Aos que a felicidade
É sol, virá a noite.
Mas ao que nada spera
Tudo que vem é grato.

210

Dia em que não gosaste não foi teu:
Foi só durares nelle. Quanto vivas
    Sem que o goses, não vives.
Não pesa que ames, bebas ou sorrias:
Basta o reflexo do sol ido na agua
    De um charco, se te é grato.
Feliz o a quem, por ter em coisas minimas
Seu prazer posto, nenhum dia nega
    A natural ventura!

211

Poisque nada que dure, ou que, durando,
Valha, neste profuso mundo obramos,
E o mesmo util para nós perdemos
    Comnosco, cedo, cedo,

O prazer do momento anteponhamos
Á absurda cura do futuro, cuja
Certeza unica é o mal presente
    Com que o seu bem compramos.

The life of those brushed by fame
Soon loses its shine.

To those for whom happiness
Is the sun, night will fall.
But for he who expects nothing
Everything that comes is pleasing.

210   [14 March 1933]
Any day that brought no pleasure was not truly yours:
You merely endured it. To experience anything
        And feel no pleasure, is not to live.
You don't have to love or drink or smile:
The reflection of the setting sun in the water
        Of a puddle is enough if it pleases you.
Happy the man to whom each day—
Because he takes pleasure in the small things—
        Brings natural happiness!

211   [16 March 1933]
Since nothing lasts or, if it does, is of no value
In the profuse world in which we labor,
And even the useful will be lost along with us
        All too soon, too soon.

Let us postpone the pleasure of the moment in favor
Of that absurd remedy, the future, whose only
Certainty is the present evil with which
        We purchase its good.

Amanhã não existe. Meu sòmente
É o momento, eu só quem existo
Neste instante, que pode o derradeiro
        Ser de quem finjo ser.

212

Estás só. Ninguem o sabe. Cala e finge.
        Mas finge sem fingires.
Nada speres que em ti já não exista,
        Cada um comsigo é tudo.
Tens sol se ha sol, ramos se ramos buscas,
        Sorte se a sorte é tua.

213

Aqui, neste miserrimo desterro
Onde nem desterrado estou, habito,
Fiel, sem que queira, àquelle antigo erro
        Pelo qual sou proscripto.

O erro de querer ser egual a alguem
Feliz, em summa—quando a sorte deu
A cada coração o unico bem
        De elle poder ser seu.

214

Uns, com os olhos postos no passado,
Vêem o que não vêem; outros, fitos
Os mesmos olhos no futuro, vêem
        O que não póde ver-se.

Tomorrow does not exist. All I have
Is this moment, and I alone exist
In this instant, which might well be the last
    For the person I pretend to be.

212   [6 April 1933]
You are alone. No one knows this. Say nothing and pretend.
    But pretend without pretending.
Expect nothing that does not already exist in you,
    We have only ourselves.
You have sun if there is sun, branches if you want branches,
    Fate if the fate is yours.

213   [6 April 1933]
Here, in this wretched place of exile
Where I am not even exiled, but live,
Involuntarily faithful to the ancient error
    That saw me banished here.

The error of wanting to be the same as someone
Happy, in short—when fate decided to give
To each heart its one and only boon,
    That of being itself alone.

214   [28 August 1933]
Some, with their eyes fixed on the past,
See what they do not see; others fix
Those same eyes on the future and see
    What cannot be seen.

Porque tam longe ir pôr o que está perto—
O dia real que vemos? No mesmo hausto
Em que vivemos, morreremos. Colhe
    O dia, porque és elle.

215

Subdito inutil de astros dominantes,
Passageiros como eu, vivo uma vida
    Que nem quero nem amo,
    Minha porque sou ella.

No ergastulo de ser quem sou, comtudo,
De em mim pensar me livro, olhando no atro
    Os astros que dominam
    Submisso de os ver bellos.

Vastidão vã que finge de infinito
(Como se o infinito se pudesse ver!)—
    Lembra-me a liberdade?
    Como, se ella a não tem?

216

Grinalda ou coroa
É só peso posto
Na fronte antes limpa.

Grinalda de rosas,
Coroa de louros,
A fronte transtornam.

Que o vento nos possa
Mexer nos cabellos,
Refrescar a fronte!

Why go so far to find what is near—
The day we can actually see? We will die
    In the same breath in which we live. Seize
        The day, because you are the day.

215   [19 November 1933]

The useless subject of dominant stars,
As fleeting as I am, I live a life
    I neither want nor love,
    Mine because I am that life.

In the prison of being who I am, though,
I step free from thinking about me by gazing into the darkness
    Where the stars rule,
    Humbled by their beauty.

A vain vastness pretending to be infinite
(As if the infinite could be seen!)—
    Does it remind me of freedom?
    How, when it is no freer than me?

216   [19 November 1933]

A garland or a crown
Is merely a weight placed
On an otherwise uncluttered brow.

Both a garland of roses,
And a crown of laurels,
Unsettle your forehead.

For the wind cannot
Ruffle your hair,
Or cool your brow!

Que a fronte despida
Possa reclinar-se,
Serena, onde durma.

Chloe! Não conheço
Melhor alegria
Que esta fronte lisa.

217
Aguardo, equanime, o que não conheço—
     Meu futuro e o de tudo.
No fim tudo será silencio, salvo
     Onde o mar banhar nada.

218
Amo o que vejo porque deixarei
     Qualquer dia de o ver.
     Amo-o tambem porque é.
No placido intervallo em que me sinto,
     Por amar, mais que ser,
     Amo o haver tudo e a mim.
Melhor me não dariam, se voltassem,
     Os primitivos deuses,
     Que tambem, nada sabem.

219
Vivem em nós innumeros;
Se penso ou sinto, ignoro
Quem é que pensa ou sente.
Sou sòmente o logar
Onde se sente ou pensa.

An unadorned forehead
Can serenely lie down
Wherever it chooses to sleep.

Ah, Chloe, I know
Of no greater joy
Than this smooth brow.

217   [15 December 1933, 5 a.m.]
I await with equanimity what I do not know—
        My future and that of all things.
Ultimately, all will be silence, except
        Where the waves break on nothing.

218   [11 October 1934]
I love what I see because one day
        I will cease to see it.
        And simply because it is.
In this placid interval in which I feel my existence,
        More because I love than because I am,
        I love both everything and myself.
They could give me nothing better were they to return,
        Those primitive gods,
        Who also know nothing.

219   [13 November 1935]
Inside us live innumerable others;
If I think or feel, I do not know
Who is thinking or feeling.
I am only the place
Where feeling and thinking happen.

Tenho mais almas que uma.
Ha mais eus do que eu mesmo.
Existo todavia
Indifferente a todos.
Faço-os callar: eu fallo.

Os impulsos cruzados
Do que sinto ou não sinto
Disputam em quem sou.
Ignoro-os. Nada dictam
A quem me sei: eu escrevo.

I have more than one soul.
There are more I's than just I myself.
And yet I remain completely
Indifferent to them all.
I silence them: I speak.

The crisscrossing impulses
Of what I feel and don't feel
Argue inside the person I am.
I ignore them. They dictate nothing
To the me I know I am: I write.

Prose

Texts to introduce Odes *(1914–1915)*

1
To Alberto Caeiro

Dear Master,
When we decided to join forces in order to begin a neoclassical renaissance in Europe, little did we know that the will of Jupiter had destined us to do so. In order to create this movement, it was necessary not only to reconstitute the ancient soul, but to give a metaphysical basis to that renaissance, because, otherwise, it would simply be a matter of transplanting pagan feeling into today's world. For us, a classical renaissance meant a continuation of the Greek tradition. And a continuation of the Greek tradition meant both a broadening out and a renewal of that same tradition, created within the eternal principles of the spirit that presides over Hellenism.

As you well know, Fate brought me into the world to take on the seemingly principal role of reintroducing the pagan soul. I need not tell you about myself, about my spontaneous self, a true and profound believer in the existence of the immortal gods. You know that, for me, Jupiter, Venus, Apollo, and the other undying presences that preside over our fleeting life are realities with a concrete existence. I am also grateful to you for having accepted so easily that I am truly a true believer in the gods. The natural response would be to find this attitude poetic. It seems strange to a modern-day man—even a believer in the god called Jesus—that he could actually coexist with someone who genuinely feels the existence of Jupiter, Apollo, the hamadryads, the nereids, the fauns, and satyrs.

What separated us, in space and life, is that thing superior to the gods themselves: Fate. However, the syncretic will of the gods continues to follow its path within us. We were brought closer by our synergistic destiny. And while you were perfecting your own new and lucid vision of the universe, taking shape in me was the whole, exiled existence of the gods, the very idea of which was the aspiration of my adolescence and a staging post on my journey into manhood.

You brought the entire Universe within each of us to the whole turbulent Portuguese literary movement. I, more humbly, Master, brought the lucid re-visioning of the gods, the rebirth of ancient beliefs, which the whole troop of false Christian gods and saints had buried.

Out of our combined efforts will doubtless be born the first impulse towards creating the New Renaissance. We have never suffered the illusion of humility, nor have we judged our art with an eye any less noble and proud than that with which Milton must have gazed upon the first pages of his *Paradise Lost*, upon the classical sculpture that is his *Samson Agonistes*. We were never taken in by the Corneilles and Racines of inferior classicism, by you, the dry, sterile materialists of our […] civilization.

We were more than aware of what an entirely sterile enterprise it would be to resurrect a classic art without first sweeping our feelings clean of all the detritus with which Christianity had covered them. No, we were never taken in by the Corneilles and the Racines. We never confused the coldness of the soul with the calm possession of our selves, nor the inability to feel with the potent, spontaneous discipline of our own feelings. Together, you instinctively and I by virtue of an education superimposed on instinct, we sloughed off the error of believing that there would be Greek classicists here from Greece or, at most, from Rome.

In this grubby, sterile, distant republic, everything is driving me towards paganism. My thoughts all turn to the calm, lucid landscape of Portugal, so naturally predestined to produce men who will receive from the remote hands of the Greeks the flame of pagan feeling.

2 [c. 1915]

The study of Italian literature, of the classic kind, also confirmed my belief that that country could continue Greece's interrupted work. In France, the writer whose soul seemed most in accord with the spirit of the pagan age was Théophile Gautier; once, when someone compared his face to that of Homer, he replied that his was, rather, that "of a sad Anacreon." In saying this, far better than I ever could, he ruled out all possibility of us considering him a classic, or of France ever reattaching her soul to a now lost Greece. And in contemporary Greece, there is nothing to indicate that the warmth of that lost beauty flows through the veins of modern-day Hellenes. Only in England, in the form of Matthew Arnold, can one find some real concept of the ancient soul. But the excessive sentiment of modern life manages to obscure the poet's essential vision. Only in one man have I clearly seen something akin to the Hellenic spirit, not culturally, but personally. That man was Eugénio de Castro.* Even though the sauce of modernity and the remnants of medieval Catholicism permeate and trammel his essentially pagan vision, there is something in him that encourages comparisons with a genuine believer in the gods, a man whose vision of Nature is filtered through a state of soul that is the legitimate sculpture in psychological form of a belief in the ancient and much-despised gods.

For the attitude that I call pagan is almost impossibly difficult to attain. It isn't enough to state that you believe in paganism (which is usually untrue), nor to feel profoundly and intensely the beauty of a Greek statue, or to intuitively understand the savor and manner of ancient life. All these things can produce a minimally pagan result in reality.

---

* Eugénio de Castro (1869–1944) was a leading Portuguese Symbolist and Decadent poet.

First, belief in the gods is a special belief, which only those who truly feel that belief today can truly understand. Intuition is not enough to enter the spirit of those lost times. We can no longer access the spiritual methods necessary to understand paganism. Belief in the gods is a faith completely different from the Christian faith. It isn't a different degree of faith, but an entirely different species. Contrary to what people might think, it is not a less intense faith, it is, in its own way, more intense. It is a faith that holds us close, that is present in us at every moment, because the gods and other near-divine presences visibly inhabit all things, and do not hide behind them. The faith of the pagan is a different belief, a different morality, and a different vision, of which no one brought up with even a lukewarm Christianity can even conceive. In the pagan faith, there is no surrender of the individual, there is no morality, no real moral feeling to trouble the pure feeling of faith. In pagan morality, there is none of the concern for the value of life taught by Christians. The common idea that paganism is a religion full of life and joy is false. Paganism is full of calm and [...]. Christianity is more human than paganism. Therein lies the superiority of paganism.

Indeed, responding intensely to a Greek statue is merely demonstrating a complete inability to understand Greek art. Feeling intensely the beauty of Greek art is a failure to understand what Greek art is. Greek art isn't meant to be felt intensely. It is purely intelligent and [...]. The element in Greek art we today call Dionysiac is an inferior element; it is what lies within Apollonian art, which dominates and directs it.

I doubtless speak of these things because I was born believing in the gods, I brought myself up in that belief, and, if they so wish, I will die in that belief. I know what pagan feeling is. I only wish I could explain how absolutely and incomprehensibly diverse it is from all our feelings. Even our serenity, and the vague stoicism some of us feel, bear no resemblance to the serenity of the ancients and of Greek stoicism.

Texts to introduce the poems of Alberto Caeiro
(1916–1924)

3   [c.1916]

So profound is his sense of the pagan soul that his poems, despite their irregular rhythm, are perfectly statuesque. It would seem, at first sight, that poems with neither rhythm nor rhyme would be incapable of giving such an overall impression of perfection. This, however, is not what happens with Caeiro's poems. They appear to be translations into human language of poems written in the language of the Gods, and which, in his version, preserve the divine equilibrium, the divine calm, the superhuman unity of works created by immortal hands.

In each line there is a lack of concern for our transient things, a curious and original scorn for the transitory, achieved through an asceticism that is aesthetic not moral, like that of the ancient Greeks, their gaze set on the beauty that does not pass and in which one forgets all about the contingent, changeable world.

The ideal of the Greeks of ancient Hellas is once again truly alive, made flesh. Once again, Olympian eyes regard the inconstant spectacle of the world. Once again, a notion of beauty is formed that has nothing to do with morality, nor is it formal, as are all the pretentious modern immoralisms, the eunuch work of such fake "aesthetes" as the Wildes, the Gautiers, and so on, whose idea of antiquity was mean and artificial.

The numerous errors inculcated in us by the example of past generations make any reformation of paganism very difficult. The man wishing to lead modern people by the hand towards Olympus must not only draw them away from the Christian path—difficult in itself—but also away from the false tracks and deviant trails along which they have been led by supposed renewers or followers of the old pagan spirit. Everything that has been said in our own days about paganism is purely formal, because it has never gone beyond a mere appearance of paganism and never grasped its real living spirit.

There were three modern interpretations of paganism, and all three misinterpreted the pagan spirit. First, there were the men of the Italian renaissance, who saw in paganism only its love of physical beauty, and its worship of formal perfection. Then came a degenerate version of this, the narrow, arid men who constituted what is known as the "classical spirit," and they saw in paganism only perfection of form, and the worship of perfection, forgetting—because normally they were true Christian spirits—the worship of beauty inherent in paganism, but of which it was, in fact, only a part. Out of that sprang the arid, sterile legions of men who, over many years, dictated the world's literary laws, the Petrarchs and the [...], the vile, aesthetic rabble of the Boileaus. In their mediocre [...] French, they took as the norm an equilibrium, a vapid rationality, ignoring the fact that, for the ancients, that equilibrium, that measure, had not been a definite thing, but a first rule of aesthetics, and therefore a limit, a brake placed on the private, unruly exuberance that exists in any sense of beauty. They failed to see that perfection is not beauty, but only a part of it, that the frontier is not the nation, but what defines it as such. (They resembled exiled emperors who erect frontiers in deserts thinking they have encompassed a vast empire because of the sheer size of the area.)

No less narrow and false, albeit in a different way, is the modern idea of paganism, which we owe to the unfortunate efforts of a sect of artists that begins with Gautier and reaches its apogee in the person of Oscar Wilde. Here the mistake is of another kind.

A Wilde is, in reality, as narrow and arid as a Boileau. It's hard to see this now, but in the distant future it will become obvious. Any mind that was born pagan will see it at once.

The last poems [of Caeiro]:

Some of them I would happily never publish. They are the fruit of an already ailing mind, in which individuality is surreptitiously betrayed by itself. They are a thought conceived in a moment of high excitement, and then left to go cold in the mind until it can be given form and shape.

I do not mean to say that the Greeks thought like the Romantics and that they performed like makers of statues. There wasn't, nor could there be, such duplicity in their minds. The act of conceiving and executing that action was already there in their mind. The way of conceiving a work of art is already the way of executing it.

4   [1916–1917]

When, almost four years ago, in Lisbon, I had occasion to show Alberto Caeiro the principles that lay behind his work, he denied any such principles. For Caeiro, absolute objectivist that he was, the pagan gods themselves were a distortion of paganism. According to his abstract objectivism, the gods were already surplus to requirements. He clearly saw that they were made in the image and likeness of material things, but they were not material things, and that was enough for him to consider them nothing at all.

For me, things have another meaning. The Greek gods represent the abstract fixation of a realizable objectivism. We cannot live without abstract ideas, because without them we cannot think. What we must do is avoid attributing to them a reality that does not derive from the material from which we take them. This is what happens to the gods. Abstract ideas have no true reality. They do, though, have a human reality, relative only to the place that the animal, man, has on the earth. The gods belong to the category of abstractions as regards their relationship with reality, but they do not belong to that category as abstractions, because they are not abstractions. Just as abstract ideas serve to guide us through things, so the gods serve to guide us through mankind. The gods are, therefore, real and unreal at the same time. They are unreal because they are not realities, but they are real because they are abstractions made real. A realized abstraction becomes pragmatically real; an unrealized abstraction is not real even pragmatically. In placing ideas in abstract people, Plato followed the old pagan process of creating gods; however, he placed his gods too far off. An idea only becomes a God when it is returned to reality. It then becomes a force of Nature. That is a God. If that is or isn't a reality, I do not know. Personally, I believe in the existence of the gods; I believe in their infinite number, in the possibility that man can ascend to being a god, and [...]

The creator of civilization is a force of Nature, and is, therefore, a god, or a demigod.

5 [c. 1917]

Alberto Caeiro is more pagan than paganism because he is more conscious of its essence than any other pagan writer. How could he be a pagan, if the essence of his psyche was conceived in opposition to a different system of sensibility, like Christianity? And when the conflict between paganism and Christianity began, during the rise of the latter, the numb and decadent mentality of the Roman people was already truly Christian, and not pagan at all. The matter becomes clear when considering Julian's attempt to react.* That emperor genuinely wanted to restore paganism, in an era—alas for him!—when the sentiment of paganism no longer existed, but only a cult of the gods where the essence of superstition was more akin to what would prove typical of Christianity than any kind of paganism.

---

* Julian (c. 331–363 CE), known as Julian the Apostate, was the last non-Christian Roman emperor. A philosopher-emperor influenced by Neoplatonism and the mystery cult of Mithras, he sought to revive classical paganism and resist the Christianization of the Empire. For Pessoa—especially in the voice of Ricardo Reis—Julian becomes the figure of the last pagan, born too late, embodying the futility of trying to reanimate a worldview whose inner life had already vanished.

Julian's own ideas reflect the inability of the times to rebuild paganism. Julian was, essentially, a Mithraist, what today would be called a theosophist or an occultist.* His attempt to rebuild paganism was, amazingly enough, based on a fusion with oriental elements that the mystic fervor of the time had made part of the spirit of the era. And thus he failed, because paganism had died, as all things die, apart, that is, from the Gods and their inscrutable tormenting knowledge.

6 [c. 1917]

I look to Caeiro's work not only for its beauty but also for its consoling aspect. For any mind that feels exiled amidst the confusion and ineptitude of contemporary life, there are moments when the weight of that difference becomes so painful that some reflection of that ancient serenity and grandeur is needed so as not to fall into the evil of despair. I have often felt, and acutely too, this feeling of being exiled among the abject things that Christianity has produced. I have never found a remedy for it among the authors of antiquity; they knew nothing of our spiritual malaise, and therefore could not write about it. They are innocent, even the most polluted of them. Reading them only exacerbates the pain that today's life causes me. It is like a child playing with me, exacerbating my adult malaise with its overly simple simplicity.

In these troubled times, the only source of consolation for my soul has been the manuscript of "The Keeper of Sheep," which I always have with me. It contains all the simplicity, all the grandeur, all the knowledge of things that the ancients had; but, having been written in opposition to the modern times that saw its birth, it offers us as balm what, in others, was only freshness; and where others barely cheered us up, like inexperienced children, this one consoles and caresses us like wise old men accustomed to excusing life.

Even if I could not feel Alberto Caeiro's work to be beautiful, I

---

* Follower of Mithraism, a mystery religion centered around the god Mithras, which was practiced in the Roman Empire from the 1st to the 4th centuries AD.

would always find it consoling. And therefore, while I did not offer them the tribute of my admiration, I could not deny them my gratitude.

Given that the two reasons for loving this work come together in my mind, for me, it stands, in my intelligence as well as in my feelings, above all other works I have read, and those include, I believe, all that is noble and serene bequeathed to us by antiquity—from the matutinal inspiration of Homer or Hesiod to the painful self-possession of an Epictetus or an Antoninus.

7 [1917–1918]

The only synthetic fact we have of experience is of external reality as a concrete reality; our mind, while it may be real, is not given to us as reality, but merely as a means of knowing reality. We do not have the right to affirm the real reality of something that is not reality but merely a means of knowing reality.

The mind has three ways of knowing reality. Certain faculties are directly involved in that knowledge: they are the faculties of perception and of reminiscence for example. Other faculties, while not involved in that knowledge, create for us ways of using it. Those are the faculties of reason. Others, the final group, serve to help us rest from reality: they are the imaginative faculties, which create another reality, which we know to be fictitious, but which delights us because it is not our day-to-day reality, and which, because it is our reality, has not been imposed on us. This way of dividing up the faculties of the mind is not mine alone; Bacon devised it and used it to support his system of classifying human and intellectual activities.

(The third group of faculties—those of the imagination—allows us to act upon reality the better to accommodate ourselves to it.) (From this come the various arts, whether those of artifice or those of the artist, to which links [...]

Images, presentations—every kind of idea that we can describe as concrete—form the substance of the first kind of activity. These ideas, more or less—in accord with perfection and the approximate normality of the brain receiving them—correspond to the real reality.

The second group of faculties, the intellectual ones, work with abstract ideas. These—as far as we know—do not correspond to any reality; that kind of thought, of which they are the substance, does not aim to reproduce reality, but rather to adapt it for us, who, being imperfect, are erroneous. Without abstract ideas there would not really be language, without which we could not communicate nor would we be human. Concrete ideas exist to give us Reality: abstract ideas to give us Utility.

The ideas, of the intermediate kind, which constitute the material of the imagination, neither correspond to reality, as concrete ideas do, nor, like abstract ideas, do they *not* correspond to it. Nor, like the former, are they innately true; nor, like the latter, are they organically false, and true only in relation to us, and to being used. They are not real because they are not channeled through the senses, through which reality comes to us; but they are not unreal, because their nature is analogous to that of the objects that the senses give us, and when we use them, they produce things that are real, as for example, when, after inventing a tool or a machine, we put it to use, and it becomes a real thing and, within other real things, a new thing. The imagination combines with the real in order to renew it in human terms. A child amusing itself by placing one stone on top of another is performing the simple act of an artist, because, albeit without realizing, it is combining real things in reality.

8 [1917–1918]

This is why Caeiro so rightly says: "Nature is parts without a whole." The Universe, as combination, synthesis and not the sum of things, is an abstract idea. That is why there is no Universe. Not because we do not know if there is or isn't one, but because we do know, that is why it is an abstract idea, which is not there.

Monotheism is a sickness of civilization, a mark of its decadence. Our monotheistic civilization was always a sick civilization.

The best example of abstract ideas and their use is numbers, mathematics. There's nothing more useful, but, in itself, nothing more false. Only a madman thinks that the number 5, for example, is *a thing*, but the number 5 is useful, as are the other numbers, because it is a means of understanding reality, not in itself, but only as regards us and our imperfection.

If our senses were perfect, we would have no need of intelligence; abstract ideas would be of no use to us at all.

The imperfection of our senses means that we can never agree on an object or an external fact. We can agree on abstract ideas though. Two men do not see a table in the same way, but both understand the word "table" in the same way. Only when trying to visualize a table will they diverge; that, though, is not an abstract idea of the table.

9 [1923–1924]

Of Alberto Caeiro I can say that he is the greatest modern poet, because, being one of the greatest of all times, he cannot help but shine too brightly in this our prolix era of inferiorities, this treacherous hour of a civilization in its death throes, a civilization that was never fully realized.

Let us set aside, right away, the first feature of these poems that immediately strikes the reader. I am referring to their abandonment of all conventional rhythmic discipline. I state from the outset that I do not agree with it. (It does not matter) … There is nothing new about this arrhythmia. From Blake's prophetic books, Southey's somber poems, those of Shelley, composed in the shadow of these, to the full flowering of free verse in Walt Whitman's books, culminating in the widespread, and rather vulgar, emphasis on this principle in our own times, free verse is neither a novelty nor is it claimed by any one school.

The only thing that can validate free verse is the rhythmic individuality that a poet can express in it. In the great practitioners—the legitimate ones that is—of free verse, the *inner tone* of the verse, its spiritual rhythm, varies from poet to poet. For the plebeian rhymer, free verse is yet another example of what should not be allowed into Parnassus.

In the free verse of a Blake or a Whitman, there is a different sound, a distinctive curve. One might say that they were written in different rhythms, although neither one nor the other is composed in what could conventionally be designated any specific kind of rhythm. Similarly, in the only great Portuguese practitioner of free verse, Senhor Álvaro de Campos, an individuality is revealed, clear and personal, in the marvelous strophic technique that emerges through the merely apparent disorder of that arrhythmia.

It's the same with Alberto Caeiro. His free verse has neither the monotonous biblical rhythm of Blake's prophetic books, nor the studiously ambling rhythm sought by Southey, Shelley, and Matthew Arnold, with intermittent success; nor Whitman's dogmatic and expansive rhythm, like a sunlit plain; nor the rhythm in Álvaro de Campos's verse, contained within the clearly symphonic concept of the Ode. Caeiro's verse is abrupt, absolutely direct, always rectilinear.

But here, if originality is shown, it is an inferior originality. Caeiro's true greatness lies in the internal structure of his poems—in the fundamentally new philosophical concept that underpins the sensibility that characterizes him.

Caeiro is, in philosophy, what no one else has been: an absolute objectivist.

He turns the poetic processes of all times upside down. I say again—of all times. He upends the philosophical processes of our era, going beyond pure knowledge in his objectivity. He breaks with all the feelings that have been the basis of poetry and human thought.

Nothing demonstrates this better than a line that is perhaps the supreme moment of his work, "Nature is parts without a whole."

Other texts (1914–1930)

10 [c. 1914]

The Return of the Gods

The gods did not die: what died was our vision of them. They did not go away: we stopped seeing them. We either closed our eyes, or some mist interposed itself between them and us. They persist, they live as they always did, with the same divinity and the same calm.

We talk a lot, and hypocritically, about the feeling we have for ancient beauty and the civilizations that were the mothers of ours, and that were pagan. But we have neither the Greek nor the Roman soul. We love them superficially, incorporeally. Nothing of the ancient soul is in us or with us. Our longing for classical beauty is entirely Christian in its fury for perfection, in its restlessness […]. The feeling we bring, in order to love them, to the pedestal of the Hellenic statues, is an insult to them. We love beauty too much: the Greeks did not love it in that way. Their feeling was imbued with the calm lucidity with which they saw. Seeing too lucidly impairs feeling too deeply. And the Greeks saw very lucidly, which is why they felt so little. Hence their perfect execution of the work of art. To execute a work of art with perfect perfection, one must not feel the beauty being sculpted too intensely. Greek art was all about balance and […]. And it was the art of those who saw and knew how to see.

We bring to the sensation of a statue the transferred feeling that Christianity taught us to bring to the adoration of Christ on the cross, a sense of moral perfection, of the ascetic and the chaste. It is not by shifting the direction of our deluded gaze that we can make it lucid and calm. We must create in ourselves a new way of seeing and feeling.

The oldest tradition of our civilization is the Greek tradition. We must return to it. We must cultivate a Greek soul within ourselves in order to continue the work of Greece. Everything since Greece has been a mistake and a deviation. Our political institutions suffer from Roman collectivism and Christian sentimentality. We mix the administrative harshness of Rome with the humanitarian softness of Christ's teachings. It is proof of how far we are from the true Greek soul.

Only science evolves. Nothing else does. Politics, arts, and customs do not evolve. They may change, but they do not evolve. Only the process of acquiring knowledge evolves, because to evolve is to grow.

There is no art but Greek art. There is no beauty but the beauty as Greece created it. We recognize this—many of us do—obscurely. In reality, our soul is so far from that that every day we betray our distant mother, [...] ancient Greece.

Our Romanism has dried us up, and our Christianity has rotted us. We have become dry and therefore weak.

We were presented with a great opportunity to reconstruct Greek civilization in a grand manner. This happened when the discoveries showed our civilization "the one and only path"—the enslavement of the black races, leading to the total aristocratization of the white races. Our Christianity interfered; we failed. But our Romanism allowed us to tame Africa, which we did not use to civilize it, or, by dominating it, to aristocratize ourselves, but purely for commerce. Today, instead of being a superior and cultured race, entirely aristocratic, we are a base mix of lowly slaves and lowly slave owners. We do not know how to command or obey; we do not know how to want or think. The Christian worm has corrupted everything inside us. Nothing changes us or raises us up.

Our lives are filled with absurdities and renunciations. We never act boldly. When we think we are doing so, it is because we are feverish. We dare feverishly, all too aware of the risks and overly intoxicated by danger. We are incomplete and infertile. We are born slaves. Our humanitarianism is a shackle we have put on ourselves. We do not know how to command. We do not know how to feel. We do not even know how to see. For over twenty centuries we have followed the wrong path, and we have not even followed it persistently.

We no longer know how to return to what we should never have left. Our Hellenism fails to grasp anything about Ancient Greece. Our love for the Roman Empire is a sickness afflicting the sickest among us. We misinterpret the perversions and crimes of past empires, imagining they are like ours. We appreciate in antiquity what we assume it has in common with us, but it has nothing in common with us. Our ignorance is profound and our [...].

We have neither progressed nor [...]. We have nothing that Antiquity did not have, and we have lost a great deal. We have gained nothing essential. Except for what science has accumulated—and could not help but accumulate—we have not progressed in any way. We have not advanced in metaphysics, art, or politics. We know as much about the essential spirit of the Universe as the Greeks did, yet we have created no beauty to surpass that of the Greeks. We have invented no system of administration and governance that equals the Greek system in producing individuals and in balancing society. Progress would have meant advances in these areas. The rest touches only the surface of our lives and gives us nothing of any true value.

Ask yourselves this question—would you rather live in the present or in Ancient Greece? I know what you would answer if you were lucid and wise. Why progress if we end up longing for the distant past rather than the present?

Yes, we have only progressed in science. And what have we truly gained with this progress? Has our knowledge really progressed? It has not: we know nothing more, essentially, about the silent center of things. Was it worth progressing because the progress of science is useful to us? Useful how, and useful in what? Because it has increased our comfort, our happiness? Do you truly believe that we are happier than the Greeks, that our life has more comfort and joy and beauty than theirs? I know you do not. So, in what have we progressed?

We move more quickly from one point to another. We exchange words more swiftly over distances. We wear fabrics that come from much farther away. But we have met without one iota more of happiness. Not a drop more knowledge cools our brow. If we delve deeply into what we know, what we have, and what we are, we will see that, as regards the world and life, our vision is no clearer or calmer, we are no happier, the fear of death weighs on us like a decree, and the bonds of sensuality still scar our bodies as they did before.

This increase in knowledge, this rise in mobility could at least have enhanced the value of the individual, given each one of us more value than among the Greeks. If there has been any change, it has been for the worse. Our rulers cannot rule; life is so complex, they stumble over so many things, even within themselves. Our artists create inferior art; there are many more than there were in the past, but what works do they produce that equal the ancient ones? Everything around us is confused and perplexed.

We are more complex, not because we have more within us, but because the eternal little we have, we possess only confusedly. Everything about us is confusion. We have lost the clear vision of the world and the clear vision of inner selves. We have become feverish and old. What is new in us, compared to what Greece had, is old age. It is old age, with its greater experience and its lesser power to use it; confused and nostalgic old age; garrulous old age, analyzing itself, its memories, its feelings, as compensation for not being able to move well, for not being able to act clearly.

We have not freed ourselves at all, in any way. Our fear has made us continue to create new gods, to whom our imposition of values gives different names. The absurd tyranny of the names "king" and "noble" has not loosened its grip on our souls. We remain slaves to preconceived ideas, fearful of ridicule, incapable of creating new methods and new visions. Deep down, everything is the same, except that sadness is more painful and uncertainty grows. Because, in our core, something like a conscience accuses us of having done nothing, of having replaced nothing we have lost. We moan loudly, like old people in pain. And in moans, and petty irritations, and actions abandoned before they are taken, our gestures grow tired, our ideas become tangled, and our lives grow weak and degraded.

Those among us who believe they are rebelling are merely reversing the yoke. Some identify as anarchists, yet they are burdened by the shackle of humanitarian sentiment brought by the Christians. Others rail against kings, others against the rich, others against [...]. But those who rail against kings do so because of the power that kings have; those who rail against the rich do so because of [...]. The yearning to be free and equal changes them like a [...].

The laws of things, however superficial, remain unknown. Who among us today could craft a rule of life that had more logic, more usefulness, more security for themselves or others? Everyone knows what they do not want, but no one knows what they want. And even what they do not want, they do not know why they do not want it, nor [...]. Our actions and thoughts are no longer simple, but neither have they become complex. They have become confused, perplexed, mere attempts at gestures, abandoned thoughts. No one has the energy to follow an idea or choose a path.

Our aims turn like weathervanes. Our ideas fall like dry leaves. Our very vices are sad and fragile. They are not born of a warm excess of life, but of a fever, a restlessness that comes from knowing that life is not enough, and the inability to imagine what would be enough.

I believe in the Gods as in a truth and a salvation. Their presence soothes and simplifies. Nothing logical leads me to prefer any other god, whether older or newer, over them. Seeing springs and forests actually inhabited by beings of another kind does not seem more absurd to me than accepting that everything came from nothing, that God is the essence of it all. And I have had the good fortune of being born with a natural sense of the presence of real beings in the forests and springs, so that, without the need for any classical preconceptions, Neptune is to me a real personality, Venus a true being, and Jupiter the terrible and living father of all the calm Gods.

Nothing helps me appreciate nature better, nor makes me love it more. The presence of a nymph brings me happiness when I am near a spring. And the company of the satyrs is welcome when I walk, humanly alone, through the serene calm of the cool forests.

The loves of the gods, their remote humanity, neither pain nor disgust me. What disgusts me is the death of a God, Christ on the cross, victim of his own father in a religion that pretends to be compassionate.

11 [1914–1915]

Eternal works are serene, lucid, and rational.

Apollo's lyre does not perish with him. It remains, so that other hands may use it to accompany new songs.

Protoplasm is not unaesthetic. It is the poets who are.

As for me, humble servant of science, I seek to study, understand, and be rational. I do not make science a goddess, nor do I speak to nature as if it were truly an entity. If I call it "she," it is because grammar compels me, as there is no neutral gender in Portuguese.

12 [c. 1915]

Metaphysical poetry is illegitimate. How can this be if metaphysics is legitimate and poetry is an intellectual product, just like metaphysics? Because poetry is not an *exclusively* intellectual product. It is based on feeling, even though it is expressed through intelligence. Intelligence should only serve to interpret the feeling. Thinking with feeling and feeling with intelligence—either of these is unhealthy.

Furthermore, "metaphysical poetry" is religious poetry. So we not only have the persistence of that unhealthy element "Religion," we also find it invading a new field, art, and for the worse too.

(regarding symbolists)
I do not wish to imply that *suggestion* be excluded from poetry. Mystery is more easily felt when *suggested* than when stated. But only mystery should be suggested.

13 [1916–1917]
General Program of Portuguese Neo-Paganism
Despite the two formulae into which the representatives of this current are divided—the formula urging the immediate revival of Hellenic paganism, and the formula in favor of simply applying it to modern conditions—Portuguese neopagans do agree on one basic approach, which is why they can form a current that, although small, is well defined. In such cases, where two divergent streams or branches form one current, their essential unity comes from having a common enemy to defeat, from a common aversion, perhaps, on which the specificity of the current is based.

Here this common aversion is the religion of Christ and its results, because they represent the civilization to which we belong.

That branch of the Portuguese neopagan current that can be designated the orthodox branch, within the concept of paganism, considers the Christian religion to be a product of Roman decadence, which took root because it represents a continuous social state. It considers Christianity in part as a mere pagan heresy, a heresy that affects the essence and not the form of faith; it also considers Christianity to be a violation of the laws of equilibrium that govern, or should govern, our civilization; it also considers it a producer of a degeneration in ideas and feelings from which our civilization's perpetually morbid state derives.

The other branch of our neopaganism accepts modern sensibility and its morbid results, recognizing them as morbid, but at the same time considering them ineradicable. Thus, instead of aspiring to or even judging to be possible a reimplantation of paganism, it believes that paganism serves only as the eternal basis of our civilization, but should serve as a discipline to the emotions created by Christianity.

We will publish, when they are ready, the two theoretical works on which Portuguese neopaganism is based, in its two divergent branches: "The Return of the Gods," by Antonio Móra* and "The Superior Paganism," by Fernando Pessoa. Before that, however, the fundamental work from which this entire movement originates will be published, especially in that branch we called orthodox—*The Keeper of Sheep, and Other Poems and Fragments,* by Alberto Caeiro (1889–1915).

Indeed, it is a real scandal that, because of our neglect, we have still not found a publisher for that work on which all of us, despite our differences, gaze with admiration. That work, the greatest poetic work of recent times, should not remain unpublished. Death, it is true, deprived us […] the work of the astonishing herald of the return of the gods, that magnificent reviver of the essence of paganism.

The branch represented solely by Fernando Pessoa believes that just as, in the end, the Christian movement was nothing but an interiorization of paganism, so, in the end, neopaganism must follow the path of Christianity, but in the true sense. While orthodox neopagans think that the "interiorization of paganism" is a meaningless phrase, since interiorizing paganism means abolishing it, Fernando Pessoa believes that the error and weakness of Christianity do not derive from the fact that it interiorized paganism, but from not knowing how to interiorize it, from having missed the path to the soul. In other words, the only way of interiorizing paganism was to discover what the inner meaning of polytheism was, what polytheism was in its subjective essence.

But what we Portuguese neo-pagans all believe in is the complete rejection of Christianity, both in its direct form, and in its indirect forms. Thus, we reject: democracy, all forms of non-aristocratic government, all humanitarian formulae, all formulae of imbalance such

* One of Pessoa's most prolific fictitious voices outside the coterie comprised of the three heteronyms (Caeiro, Campos, Reis). Mora came onto the scene in 1915.

as, for example, German imperialism or allied democracy; we reject feminism, because it aims to make women equal to men and grant women political and social rights, when women are inferior beings only necessary to humanity for the essential but merely biological fact of its continuation; we reject soppy anti-scientific trends, such as vegetarianism, anti-alcoholism, anti-vivisectionism, giving rights to animals inferior to man. We reject the pacifist principle; we reject modern imperialisms, all of a Catholic nature—the whole Holy Roman Empire that every England or every Germany secretly wants to be; we reject [...]

In this, we are all in agreement ...

We reject the idiotic Spartanism of eugenicists, and the machine-like improvement of races. We reject the traditionalist formula, because the only true civilized tradition is the pagan tradition: the others are local traditions devoid of any civilizing effect, harmful to nations. A conservative people is a dead people.

14 [c. 1930]

A poem is the projection of an idea into words through emotion. Emotion is not the basis of poetry; it is merely the means that the idea employs to translate itself into words.

I do not see the fundamental difference between poetry and prose, peculiar to the disposition of the mind, that Campos sets out. Using words means using an instrument that is both emotional and intellectual. The word contains both an idea and an emotion. Thus, there is no prose, not even the most rigidly scientific, that does not carry some emotional essence. Similarly, there is no exclamation, not even the most abstractly emotive, that does not imply at least the outline of an idea.

One might argue, for example, that a pure exclamation—"Ah," for instance—contains no intellectual element. However, there is no "ah," written in isolation, that bears no relation to something preceding it. Either we consider the "ah" as spoken, with the tone of voice conveying the feeling that animates it, and thus the idea linked to that feeling; or the "ah" responds to a phrase, or is formed by it, and manifests an idea provoked by that phrase.

In everything that is expressed—poetry or prose—there is both idea and emotion. Poetry differs from prose only in that it chooses an additional external means, beyond the word, to convey the idea in words through emotion. This means can be rhythm, rhyme, stanza, or all three, or two, or just one. However, I do not believe it can be less than one.

The idea, in using emotion to express itself in words, shapes and defines that emotion. Rhythm, rhyme, or stanza are the projection of this shape—the affirmation of the idea through an emotion that, if not shaped by the idea, would overflow and lose its very capacity for expression.

This, in my view, is what happens in Campos's poems. They are an overflow of emotion. The idea serves the emotion, it does not dominate it. And the man—whether poet or not—in whom emotion dominates intelligence, is shifting the configuration of his being back to earlier stages of evolution, where the faculties of inhibition still lay dormant in the embryo of the mind. Art, which is a product of culture, that is, the supreme development of man's self-awareness, cannot be deemed to be superior the more closely it resembles the mental manifestations that distinguish the earlier stages of cerebral evolution.

Poetry is superior to prose because it does not express a higher degree of emotion, but, *per contra*, a higher degree of control over it, subordinating the tumult in which emotion would naturally be expressed (as Campos correctly states) to rhythm, rhyme, and stanza.

Since the mental state in which poetry is formed is indeed more emotive than that in which prose is naturally formed, it is necessary to apply a stricter discipline to the poetic state than to the prosaic state of mind. And those devices—rhythm, rhyme, stanzas—are the tools of such discipline.

In the sense that Campos considers rhythm, rhyme, and stanza to be artifices, one can say that the will that corrects flaws, the order that polices societies, and the civilization that reduces egotism to a sociable form are also artifices.

In the most properly prosaic prose—be it scientific or philosophical—which directly expresses ideas and only ideas, there is no need for great discipline, since the very act of dealing solely with ideas provides sufficient discipline. In more broadly emotive prose, such as that which distinguishes oratory or has a descriptive nature, more attention must be paid to rhythm, arrangement, and organization of ideas, as these are fewer and do not form the basis of the material. In highly emotive prose—the kind whose feelings could just as easily be expressed in poetry—there must be even greater attention to the organization of material and the accompanying rhythm of the exposition. This rhythm is not as defined as it is in verse, because prose is not verse. What Campos is actually doing, when he writes in verse, is writing rhythmic prose with greater pauses marked at certain points for rhythmic purposes, and these greater pauses he determines by the endings of the lines. Campos is a great prose writer, with a profound understanding of rhythm; but the rhythm he understands is that of prose, and the prose he employs includes, beyond the usual punctuation marks, a longer, special pause, which he, like his predecessors, chose to represent graphically with a broken line at the end, arranged like a verse. If Campos, instead of doing this, had invented a new punctuation mark—say the vertical stroke (/)—to indicate this type of pause, making it clear that there is a pause similar to the one at the end of a verse, he would not have created a different work, nor caused the confusion he did.

Discipline can be natural or artificial, spontaneous or reflective. What distinguishes classical art—the art of the Greeks and even the Romans—from pseudo-classical art, like that of the French during their centuries of rigidity, is that the discipline of the former resides in the very emotions—with a natural harmony of the soul—that instinctively repel excess, even when feeling it; whereas the discipline of the latter resides in a conscious decision of the mind not to feel beyond a certain level. Pseudo-classical art is cold because it is governed by rules; classical art contains emotion because it is governed by harmony.

It almost follows from what Campos says that an ordinary poet feels spontaneously with the expansiveness that would naturally appear in verses such as he writes; and then, upon reflection, would subject that emotion to cuts, retouches, and other mutilations or alterations, in obedience to an external rule. No man has ever been a poet in such a manner. The discipline of rhythm is learned until it becomes part of the soul: the verse that emotion produces is born already subordinate to that discipline. A naturally harmonious emotion is a naturally ordered emotion; a naturally ordered emotion is naturally translated into an ordered rhythm, for the emotion provides the rhythm and the order within it, the order that exists in the rhythm.

With words, intelligence provides the phrase, and emotion provides the rhythm. When the poet's thought is elevated, that is, formed from an idea that produces an emotion, this thought, inherently harmonious given the balanced union of idea and emotion, and by the nobility of both, transmits this balance of emotion and feeling to the phrase and the rhythm. Thus, as I have said, the phrase, subject to the thought that defines it, seeks it out, and the rhythm, slave to the emotion that the thought has gathered to itself, serves it.